Capital, Labour
and the
Middle Classes

NICHOLAS ABERCROMBIE
JOHN URRY

Department of Sociology, University of Lancaster

London
GEORGE ALLEN & UNWIN
Boston   Sydney

George Allen & Unwin (Publishers) Ltd,
40 Museum Street, London WC1A 1LU, UK

George Allen & Unwin (Publishers) Ltd,
Park Lane, Hemel Hempstead, Herts HP2 4TE, UK

Allen & Unwin, Inc.,
9 Winchester Terrace, Winchester, Mass. 01890, USA

George Allen & Unwin Australia Pty Ltd,
8 Napier Street, North Sydney, NSW 2060, Australia

First published in 1983
Second impression 1984

British Library Cataloguing in Publication Data

Abercrombie, Nicholas
   Capital, labour and the middle classes. −
(Controversies in sociology series; 15)
1. Middle classes
I. Title   II. Urry, John   III. Series
305.5′5   HT650
ISBN 0-04-301145-4
ISBN 0-04-301146-2   Pbk

Library of Congress Cataloging in Publication Data

Abercrombie, Nicholas
   Capital, labour and the middle classes.
(Controversies in sociology; 15)
Bibliography: p.
Includes index.
1. Middle classes. 2. Proletariat 3. Social classes.
I. Urry, John.   II. Title   III. Series.
HT684.A23 1983   305.5′5   83-3830
ISBN 0-04-301145-4
ISBN 0-04-301146-2   Pbk

Set in 10 on 11 point Times by Red Lion Setters, London, WC1
and printed in Great Britain by Billing and Sons Ltd, London and Worcester

Contents

Acknowledgements

We are very grateful to Stephen Hill, Roger King, Scott Lash, John Trevitt and Alan Warde for their comments on earlier drafts of this book, and to the Sociology Department at Lancaster University for more general encouragement and inspiration. We are also indebted to Maeve Conolly, Wendy Francis and Heather Salt for struggling and re-struggling with the manuscript and eventually turning it into typescript.

We are also grateful to the following for permission to reprint tabular material: Macmillan Publishers Ltd., for Tables 1.1 and 1.2, reprinted from G. Routh, *Occupation and Pay in Great Britain*; Humanities Press Inc., for Table 1.3, reprinted from J. Gershuny, *After Industrial Society*.

1

The Problem of the Middle Classes

In this book we shall consider how to analyse one of the most intractable issues in contemporary sociology: what is the class position of that class or classes which is or are in some sense intermediate between labour and capital? We shall survey most of the major recent contributions to such an analysis in the first part of the book; and in the second we shall discuss certain issues raised by this literature in further detail. We do not presume to solve all of these issues here but we do think that we make certain advances in three areas: first, in analysing the differentiation between what we will term the 'service class' and 'deskilled white-collar workers'; secondly, in considering the crucial significance of knowledge, science and education for the constitution of such classes; and thirdly, in investigating some of the important social effects of the development of such classes in modern capitalism. Overall, we believe that classes are to be viewed as entities possessing causal powers and that sociological investigation has to examine the interdependence between these different social forces which possess such powers. We think that much class analysis, which involves the classification of individuals and groups, is relatively less important than analysing the forms of interdependence and struggle, both between classes and between other distinctive social forces – considering, in other words, the respective causal powers of the entities under investigation.

We shall also argue that there is something distinctive about the middle classes within contemporary capitalism and that it is therefore incorrect to treat the contemporary middle classes as direct descendants of the eighteenth- or nineteenth-century variants. Thus, when the Rev. Thomas Gisborne first employed the term in 1785 he used it to refer to the propertied and largely entrepreneurial class located between landowners on the one hand, and urban-industrial workers and agricultural labourers on the other, in a society undergoing transition (Bradley, 1975). Modern day uses of the 'middle class' vary considerably (see Chapters 2, 3, 4 and 5 below), but in general the term refers to various 'white-collar occupations', from higher professionals to relatively routine clerical workers. The sociological issues have mainly revolved around the divisions between such groupings and the capitalist class, on the one hand, and the working class, on the other. In this introductory chapter, we shall, first, detail the main occupational changes that are involved within the sphere of 'white-collar work'; secondly, we shall consider various issues which revolve around both the boundaries between classes, and the fragments within the middle classes; and thirdly, we shall summarise the two main theoretical frameworks involved in the investigation of such classes, the Weberian and the Marxist. We shall use the generic term 'middle classes' throughout much of this book, although in Part Two we shall in fact suggest that neither of the important 'middle classes' is strictly speaking 'in the middle', and only one is to be viewed as a 'class'.

THE CHANGING COMPOSITION OF WHITE-COLLAR
OCCUPATIONS

The phenomenon that has provoked sociological interest in the middle classes has been the growth of white-collar occupations (see Table 1·1). The most noticeable shift in the period 1911−71 was the steep decline in classes 5−7 (manual workers) and the growth of foremen and the three white-collar categories − clerks, employers and managers, and professionals. Over the years 1911−71, classes 5−7 lost over 21 per cent of the total employed population, made up of 6·5 per cent to professionals, over 2 per cent to managers and employers, 9 per cent to clerks, and over 2·5 per cent to foremen. The white-collar categories themselves did not all gain equally. The higher professional group more than tripled in size, managers rather more than doubled, while the size of the employer group declined. The rate of growth of white-collar occupations also varied over time. The growth in the clerical grade, for example, was at its highest in the years 1911−21, while the higher professional category increased most quickly between 1951 and 1971 (see Routh, 1980, p. 8).

For both men and women there was a shift out of manual work into white-collar occupations. However, the movement out of manual work was greater for women (30 per cent) than for men (16 per cent). Significantly, for women, clerical work was disproportionately the recipient of the outflow from manual work; indeed, the proportion of men employed as clerks hardly increased between 1911 and 1971. As far as the other categories of non-manual work are concerned, the increase in male managers, and higher and lower professionals, was considerably greater than for their female equivalents.

Some further light is thrown on these differences by Table 1·2, which shows the gender composition of the white-collar occupational groupings. The higher professional category is overwhelmingly male, and there has been less change in this area of employment than in any other. In the lower professions, an initial preponderance of women in 1911 had been turned into a position of more or less parity by 1971, largely through the disproportionate recruitment of male teachers. Similarly, the proportion

Table 1.1 *Occupational Class of the Gainfully Employed Population in Great Britain (%)*

		All					Men					Women			
		1911	1921	1931	1951	1971	1911	1921	1931	1951	1971	1911	1921	1931	1951	1971
1	Professional															
	A Higher	1·00	1·01	1·14	1·93	3·29	1·34	1·36	1·50	2·56	4·87	0·20	0·18	0·29	0·52	0·55
	B Lower	3·05	3·52	3·46	4·70	7·78	1·61	2·02	2·03	3·16	5·95	6·49	7·07	6·83	8·18	10·95
2	Employers and Managers															
	A Employers	6·71	6·82	6·70	4·97	4·22	7·74	7·69	7·65	5·74	5·07	4·28	4·74	4·44	3·22	2·75
	B Managers	3·43	3·64	3·66	5·53	8·21	3·91	4·28	4·54	6·78	10·91	2·30	2·11	1·60	2·73	3·51
3	Clerical Workers	4·84	6·72	6·97	10·68	13·90	5·48	5·40	5·53	6·35	6·38	3·30	9·90	10·34	20·41	27·00
4	Foremen	1·29	1·44	1·54	2·62	3·87	1·75	1·91	2·00	3·28	5·04	0·18	0·32	0·45	1·14	1·84
5–7	Manual Workers	79·67	76·85	76·53	69·58	58·23	78·17	77·32	76·73	72·12	61·79	83·25	75·68	76·05	63·81	53·40

Source: Adapted from Routh, 1980, table 1.1; Register General's categories.

of women managers also declined over the period. The sex composition of the clerical grade, on the other hand, was almost reversed. While almost 80 per cent of clerks were men in 1911, 70 per cent were women in 1971.

Not only were there significant movements between classes, there were also important changes within them. In the higher professions for example, the numbers of engineers increased by seventeen times between 1911 and 1971, while scientists were fifteen times as strongly represented, and accountants were seven times as numerous. The traditional professions, law, medicine and the military, only doubled their numbers, while the number of clergy declined. The lower professions were dominated by government service. Teachers and nurses alone accounted for 57 per cent of the class in 1911 and 58 per cent in 1971. Social welfare workers and laboratory technicians increased some twentyfold in the same sixty years, while the numbers of teachers and nurses only quadrupled, an increase which included a striking growth in the numbers of male teachers and nurses.

These changes in occupational distributions may have been due either to changes in the distribution within industries, or to the growth or contraction of industries (see discussion in Routh, 1980, pp 40–4). As far as higher and lower professionals are concerned, the growth of industries has been more important in explaining their growth than changes in their proportions within each industry. For clerks, the reverse was true until 1951, after which the growth of industries typically employing a high proportion of clerks became a more significant factor.

The importance of newer, more 'white-collar' industries has led some commentators to speculate on the possibility that this represents a shift from an economy based on the production of goods to one based on the production of services. Gershuny (1978) has investigated the relationship of tertiary occupations (clerical, sales, services, administration, professional and technical) to primary, intermediate and secondary industries (mining, farming, manufacturing, transport, utilities and construction). By 1971 more than half the working population were employed in tertiary occupations. However, Gershuny argues, this conceals the degree to which many of those in tertiary occupations were employed either in manufacturing industry or in 'goods-related industry (distribution, banking, insurance, and finance)'.

Table 1·3 shows the effects of breaking down tertiary occupations by type of industry. Only 46 per cent of those in tertiary occupations were engaged in the provision of services, representing 23·9 per cent of the working population. Indeed, even this is an overestimate, since a proportion of the technical and professional occupations, while not employed directly in manufacturing or goods-related industries, still contributed to the production of goods: computer programmers, for example. Indeed, only a minority of white-collar workers were employed in directly providing consumer services.

Table 1.2 Sex Composition of Certain Occupations (Registrar General's Categories 1–3) (%)

	Men					Women				
	1911	1921	1931	1951	1971	1911	1921	1931	1951	1971
1 Professional										
A Higher	94·02	95·54	92·50	91·94	93·93	5·97	5·13	7·50	8·29	6·07
B Lower	37·14	40·59	41·21	46·46	48·61	62·86	59·26	58·79	53·54	51·39
2 Employers and Managers										
A Employers	81·17	79·51	80·13	79·96	76·23	18·83	20·49	19·73	19·95	23·77
B Managers	80·45	82·95	87·01	84·75	84·37	19·87	17·05	12·99	15·17	15·63
3 Clerical Workers	79·82	56·62	55·77	41·18	29·12	20·18	43·38	44·23	58·82	70·88

Source: Calculated from Routh, 1980, table 1.1.

Table 1.3   *Tertiary Occupations and their Employment, 1961–71*

		1961	1971	$\dfrac{1971}{1961}$
Clerical	Manufacturing	6·0	6·0	1·00
	Goods-related	3·4	4·2	1·24
	Services-related	3·9	4·7	1·20
Sales	Manufacturing	0·9	0·9	1·00
	Goods-related	8·4	7·9	0·99
	Services-related	0·5	0·5	1·00
Services	Manufacturing	1·4	2·1	1·50
	Goods-related	0·5	0·8	1·40
	Services-related	8·7	10·1	1·16
Administration	Manufacturing	1·9	2·5	1·32
	Goods-related	0·3	0·6	2·00
	Services-related	0·6	0·8	1·33
Professional and technical	Manufacturing	2·5	3·2	1·28
	Goods-related	0·5	0·5	1·00
	Services-related	6·0	7·8	1·30

Source: Gershuny, 1978, p. 102.

BOUNDARIES, FRAGMENTS AND PROLETARIANISATION

Sociological interpretations of the findings described in the previous section vary a great deal, as we shall demonstrate. One conclusion that is regularly drawn in that contemporary industrial capitalist societies generally, and their middle classes in particular, are becoming much more heterogeneous and differentiated. There are more occupations that are described as middle class, with a greater range of skills, qualifications and earnings. The middle classes, in other words, are becoming fragmented. This fragmentation, in turn, generates a number of theoretical problems. With a class characterised by a great diversity of condition of its members, it becomes difficult to decide who is a member of that class and who is not, a difficulty which we shall refer to as the Boundary Problem. Decisions as to where the boundaries of the class lie become relatively arbitrary. Solutions to this problem vary considerably, and many sociologists may not even recognise it as a problem. Thus some writers simply break up the array of occupations into various categories which they call classes. Others reply that the categories thus created lack sociological meaning and that some criterion such as 'relationship to the means of production' is required which will produce relatively unambiguous class boundaries. In the case of the middle class, uncertainty over where to place the boundaries of the class is most acute at the point where it overlaps with the working class. Indeed, the possibility that certain occupations, chiefly those involving routine white-collar work, are becoming indistinguishable from manual, working-class occupations in all important respects dominates most discussions of the middle class. Again, opinions about the degree and meaning of the proletarianisation of middle-class occupations vary considerably, as we shall show in later chapters.

A treatment of these issues is an essential part of any sociological theory of the middle class and theories can be classified according to the different views that they take of these questions. For example, many theories that stress the fragmentation of the middle classes also propose theories of their proletarianisation, and recognise that there is a problem of establishing that there are boundaries with other classes. By contrast, alternative theories stress the relative coherence of the middle class, emphasise its sociological importance and reject the proletarianisation thesis.

Such theories have a variety of intellectual debts. The conventional way of classifying theories of social class is in terms of the distinction between Weberian and Marxist approaches. We shall now discuss some recent debates and distinctions drawn by various 'Weberian' and 'Marxist' writers.

WEBERIAN AND MARXIST THEORIES OF CLASS

The claim that Weber and Marx founded different traditions within sociology has frequently been made. Within the theory of stratification the contrast is thought to be particularly sharp. Bottomore (1965), for example, argues that Marx affirmed 'the economic basis of classes' which in turn meant the increasing separation and polarisation of the bourgeoisie and the proletariat. Weber, on the other hand, in presenting 'a comprehensive alternative' to the Marxist theory, argued that stratification by prestige, based on occupation, consumption and style of life, is particularly important in capitalist societies. This form of status stratification produces a hierarchy of continuously graded positions based on a variety of factors, not just the ownership of productive property. On this view, it is impossible to conceive of the class system of contemporary capitalist societies as consisting of two opposed classes.

This Weberian conception of status stratification has been most developed by a number of American writers. For Warner (1960), for example, status and class are more or less synonymous terms. 'Something more than a large income is necessary for high social position. Money must be translated into socially approved behaviour and possessions, and they in turn must be translated into intimate participation with, and acceptance by, members of a superior class' (p. 21). For Warner, the class system is equivalent to the status system, which is in turn a function of the perceptions and evaluations of the participants in the system, not of the 'objective' characteristics of occupation, income, or property.

The essence of this 'Weberian' critique of Marxism is that it makes the economy the most important determinant of the class structure but, in doing so, it neglects the equally critical, or more important, role of status stratification and style of life. 'Status' is counterposed to 'economy'.

However, in recent British sociology the debate between Marxist and Weberian positions has been renewed by a revival of interest in Marx's political economy. This debate is different from the earlier one in two ways. First, it has been initiated by Marxists who have criticised what they take to be Weberian positions, rather than by Weberians who have found fault with Marxist economic determinism. Secondly, the basis of the debate is no longer a perceived contrast between economic determinants and status divisions. Rather, it is suggested that both Marxist and Weberian theorists stress the importance of the economic level in the determination of social classes, but they differ as to the constitution of the economy (see Hill, 1981).

A definite and forceful statement of this point of view is provided by Crompton and Gubbay (1977; and also see Crompton, 1976, and Benson, 1978). They argue that Weber's conception of class depends on the notion of life-chances, that is, on the opportunities to acquire rewards. Individuals with similar life-chances occupy the same class situation. In turn, life-chances are determined by the individual's relationship to markets of various kinds, including those of property and types of labour. It is true, as Crompton and Gubbay concede, that Weber's introduction of the concept of status would appear to interfere with the equation of class situation with market situation. Weber suggested that, although in times of rapid social change the market, and therefore class stratification, will predominate, in more settled times life-chances will be mainly determined by non-economic, status considerations. None the less, despite the possibility that Weber believes that life-chances, and hence class, are determined by both economic and non-economic factors, Crompton and Gubbay conclude, rather arbitrarily and weakly, that a clearer interpretation is that, for Weber, class situation should be identified with market situation.

Marx, on the other hand, cannot be interpreted as believing that market situation is fundamental to class determination. This is not because he rejects economic determinism. It is rather, according to Crompton and Gubbay, because the category of market situation is not fundamental enough. For Marx, in the market for labour buyers and sellers are equals, exchanging equivalent commodities. The worker obtains what his labour is 'worth'. Apparently paradoxically, however, Marx also holds that there is a relation of exploitation between seller and buyer. The resolution of the paradox lies in the notion that there is, underlying equal market relations, a more fundamental relationship that *is* exploitive. The key to this more fundamental relationship is the supposition that labour-power, when put to work, creates value greater than the value expended in buying it, that is, its wages. The relationship between the labourer and the capitalist is exploitive, simply because this surplus value is appropriated by the capitalist while it is created by the worker. This view of the way in which value is produced generates a model of the class structure in which there are two classes. The proletariat, since it does not own or control productive resources, is forced to sell its labour-power. The bourgeoisie does own and control the means of production, directs labour-power and appropriates the surplus product. This two-class model is, however, an abstract scheme that displays the basic structure of capitalist societies. A more complex model than this will be required which will accommodate groups that do not immediately fit into either the proletariat or the bourgeoisie.

Marx and Weber, therefore, on this account, have quite different theories of class.

> Marx, unlike Weber, did not perceive class relationships as being structured through a system of market exchange. Rather Marx's analysis directs attention to the unequal social relationship underlying the 'fair' exchange of the market – the process by which the employer obtains labour-power, the use of which facilitates the creation of surplus value. Logically, therefore, Marx's analysis focuses upon relationships of production, rather than relationships of exchange. (Crompton and Gubbay, 1977, p. 14)

Weberian theory concentrates on how classes are produced as a result of the manner in which rewards are acquired and distributed; Marxist theory emphasises the way in which particular social relations within production create and reproduce social classes.

For Crompton and Gubbay, most analyses of the class structure in British sociology are Weberian in inspiration. This characteristic does not necessarily make them incorrect. Since production relations underlie market relations, analysis which concentrates on the latter will be merely incomplete or, at worst, misleading. For example, if class is defined in terms of market opportunities, then interpretation of class conflict must centre on the struggles between groups over access to the market. This will, however, neglect the more fundamental mechanisms which control such access. The existence of the market is simply taken for granted, rather than treated as a phenomenon requiring explanation. It is the social relationships involved in the capitalist mode of production that explain market relations and so provide the fundamental basis for research on the class structure. (For further discussion of Marxist theories of class, see Chapters 4 and 5.)

Besides being distinctive in providing a particularly forthright statement of the contrast between Marxist and Weberian theories, Crompton and Gubbay's work is part of a more general and influential theoretical tendency. Johnson (1977a), for example, similarly argues that the Weberian solutions dominant in sociology are inadequate for the analysis of the middle class. Two features of these solutions particularly attract his attention. First, the Weberian focus on life-chances in relation to a market does not provide a clear means of distinguishing one class from another, and the distribution of life-chances in a society forms a continuous array without clear breaks. Imposing a class structure on this array is an arbitrary exercise. Secondly, explanations of changes in the class structure, in particular the appearance of the middle class, tend to focus on the growth of rational-legal bureaucratic organisation designed to cope with the administrative problems of the increasing division of labour. In Johnson's view, these two features of Weberian theory tend to mislead, in that both neglect the determining importance of the underlying social relationships of the mode of production. In the case of the first feature, the important one from our point of view, the marketability of skills is a function of a specific mode of production: 'any attempt to identify a social class must initially theoretize class relationships at the level of production rather than distribution which is itself an outcome of the mode of production' (Johnson, 1977a, p. 105). Much the same point, though round a different set of issues, is made in a more recent debate between Crompton (1980) and Goldthorpe (1980a). In questioning some of the findings of the Oxford mobility study, Crompton argues, in effect, that mobility between *occupations* does not necessarily say anything about changes in the class structure. The implication is that occupation – a 'market' category – and class must be defined independently of one another; class is not reducible to occupation. Thus, over time, it is possible for occupations to change their class location.

In sum, the Marxist critique of Weberianism concentrates on the latter's emphasis upon relations in the market rather than relations of production. The suggestion is that, since production is 'logically prior' to distribution, successful theories of the class structure must ultimately refer to the particular features of the capitalist mode of production. There has, very recently, been some Weberian response to these changes, a response the more significant because it seems to accept the terms of the debate. Parkin (1979), for example, tends to agree with Crompton and Gubbay's characterisation of Weberian theories as grounded in phenomena of distribution and Marxist theories as emphasising relations of production and the 'inbuilt antagonism between capital and labour'. However, the Marxist view that the 'concealed forces of the productive system' underlie, explain and govern the patterns of distribution does not convince him. He says:

> The Marxist preoccupation with the realm of production, increasingly held up as its mark of theoretical rigour, obscures from view any recognition of the possibility that some line of cleavage other than that between

capital and labour could constitute the primary source of political and social antagonism. To accept that social inequalities and injustices stemming from racial, religious, linguistic, and sexual divisions could have a reality *sui generis*, not reducible to causes buried deep in the capitalist mode of production, would look suspiciously like a Weberian approach with all its peculiar fascination for distributive patterns and outcomes. (Parkin, 1979, p. 5).

Parkin's basic point is, therefore, that the Marxist concept of the mode of production does not have the explanatory power that Crompton and Gubbay or Johnson would wish to ascribe to it. It cannot adequately account for the complex social divisions of contemporary societies and, more narrowly, distributive arrangements cannot be read off from the characteristics of a productive system. Distributive arrangements are crucial and, as Parkin says elsewhere, 'the backbone of the class structure, and indeed of the entire reward system of modern Western society, is the occupational order' (1972, p. 18).

A number of writers on stratification therefore conspire in a particular view of the relationship of Marxist and Weberian theories of class. However, we shall argue in Chapter 6 that, for a number of reasons, this relationship is a good deal more complex than is presented and that any satisfactory theory of class has to solve theoretical problems that are common to both points of view. None the less, the distinction between two schools of analysis does have exegetical value in discussing the views of writers on the middle classes and we shall employ it as far as it is possible to do so in the next four chapters. Part of our purpose here will be to assess the thesis that there is incompatibility between Weberian and Marxist analyses of the middle classes (a doctrine which we shall call the Incompatibility Thesis).

In these next four chapters, Part One, we shall consider the main approaches to the middle classes, discussing first Weberian and then Marxist accounts. In Part Two we shall take up certain issues in greater detail arguing *inter alia* that, in considering the middle classes in particular, the alleged distinction between these forms of analysis collapses.

Part One

Contrasting Approaches to the Middle Classes

2
Some Weberian Theories of the Middle Classes

The Weberian literature available on the middle class is immense. In reviewing it we must necessarily be selective and we have adopted the strategy of considering separately and in detail a number of important works which deal either directly or indirectly with the middle class, and then, in a separate chapter, discussing a number of themes that are characteristic of Weberian analysis in general.

MILLS ON WHITE-COLLAR WORKERS

Mills's (1951) book is important because it was one of the earliest self-consciously sociological studies of the middle class in English. It is not written with lengthy theoretical disquisitions in the European style and the result is a loosely related assembly of bits of discussion, at times almost anecdotal and speculative. What holds it together is a particular 'frame of mind' not uncommon in American writings of a certain genre (see, for example, Braverman, 1974). Thus, in *White Collar*, a major theme is the experience of being middle class, of being a salesperson, office worker, or lawyer. Allied with this stress on the experimental is a concern with certain populist, mass society themes. There is a concentration on the growth of bureaucracy in all areas of life, from business to education and from law to the arts. Further, Mills argues that mechanisation, and its consequent deskilling, have led to a reduction in the quality of work experience.

For Mills, the origins of the class of alienated white-collar workers lie in the decisive break between the old entrepreneurial society and the new bureaucratised order. The critical difference between the two types of society lies in the way in which property, and more particularly productive property, is owned. Generally, productive property is not privately owned by single persons or families; it is no longer the case that the legal owners of businesses direct and control them. However, this does not mean that private property is irrelevant to the exercise of managerial functions for, ultimately, the right to head the chain of command does depend on the right of property ownership.

However, although the function of individual property ownership has not been lost, it has been transformed, for the institutionalisation and depersonalisation of property has ramifications for the class structure. The 'middle class' no longer consists of entrepreneurs who own the enterprises that they control. It consists of propertyless workers in certain occupations which have greatly expanded in number over the past hundred years. It is not clear here in what sense the 'old' middle class and the 'new' middle class are both middle or are continuous over time. More important, the claim that the mechanism of the transformation in the nature of the middle class was a change in property relations is misleading. Indeed, Mills goes on to give more specific, and different, reasons for the growth of new middle-class occupations. First, technological changes have resulted in greater labour productivity. As a consequence, far fewer productive workers are needed. Secondly, large-scale enterprise has needed large-scale marketing and distribution. Hence, there has been an increase in the numbers of people involved in selling, transportation, communication and in those financial sectors to do with merchandising, credit-financing and banking. Thirdly, the growth in the size of businesses and the very much greater scope of government activities has meant an increased demand for people to co-ordinate, administer and manage. Mills suggests that these are changes in the *occupational* structure. At times he appears to argue that the factors producing occupational changes and the transformation of property relations are independent processes. The former is engineered by the 'industrial mechanics' of society while the latter is rather an index (not a cause) of a shift in the basis of stratification. It is occupation, rather than property, that is the basis of class stratification in contemporary societies.

Mills is thus unequivocally, and explicitly, Weberian in his emphasis on the occupational order as the basis of class. He also, unlike many of his contemporaries, makes a clear conceptual distinction between class and status. However, although class and status are conceptually separate, they are empirically connected, and Mills argues that the social esteem claimed by white-collar groups, and expressed in their style of life, is one of their defining characteristics, though secondary to class. Mills's definition of the class position of white-collar workers in terms of occupation and chances in the labour market raises the Boundary Problem discussed in Chapter 1. Where does the middle class begin and end? In what sense do various occupations with slightly different chances in the market share a common class position? Mills does not satisfactorily answer these questions and the problem is compounded by a number of points that Mills makes. For example, in stressing the point that the middle classes are propertyless, he simultaneously demonstrates their similarity to the propertyless working classes. At the same time, he emphasises the fragmented nature of the middle class, a conclusion reinforced by the manner in which he separately discusses the position and experience of the middle-class occupations.

Although the heterogeneity and fragmentation of the middle class may create theoretical difficulties in terms of the definition, location and determinants of that class, for Mills these features are simply brute facts of contemporary societies; facts, moreover, with an important bearing on the consequences of the existence of the middle class. Particularly significant here are its political activities. Mills notes that the presence of a middle class makes some traditional theories of class conflict seem oversimplified since the middle class not only appears as an intermediary, it also further diversifies the propertyless. It is, moreover, itself an 'occupational salad' with no political unity. In sum, the middle class makes social analysis more complicated, and Mills finds that it is not easy to show what factors determine its political posture. In his view, the objective, structural position of the middle class is coming closer to that of the working class in respect of income, propertylessness and levels of skill. In this sense the white-collar worker is becoming proletarianised, and this is reflected in some political ways – for example, in increased union membership. However, proletarianisation of this kind is no guide to the politics of the middle class which may continue to stress the separation from the working class. Furthermore, the familiar fragmentation of the middle class prevents any coherent politics other than political indifference or a tendency to support whatever political interest is in the ascendant. 'For these classes are diversified in social form, contradictory in material interest, dissimilar in ideological illusion; there is no homogeneity of base among them for common political movement' (Mills, 1951, p. 351).

In rejecting what he refers to as Marxist economic determinism, Mills introduces a certain indeterminacy. It is not clear how, for Mills, the middle class is a *class*, or what factors produce any particular form of politics. He does not, in other words, show why the various middle-class occupations have similar life-chances. It should be said that Mills does not have the resolution of these theoretical difficulties as his main aim. This is both because he is not intending to write a work of theory, and also because he is working within a particular American tradition and writing about American society, with its lack of mass working-class organisation and the importance of entrepreneurial ideology. The next text that we shall consider is in many ways the reverse of this, being strongly 'European' in its theoretical orientation.

DAHRENDORF ON CLASS AND CLASS CONFLICT

Dahrendorf's (1959) aim is not primarily the elucidation of the class position of the middle class, or even of the class structure as a whole, but of the bases of class conflict. Conflict is important, not only in itself, but because it effects changes in the social structure. Clearly the questions of class formation and class action are linked, but Dahrendorf is insistent that they are analytically separate and should be discussed independently, and the bulk of his book is directed to examining the conditions of conflict itself. Because our own discussion has other aims we shall not examine his whole argument but only those parts of it germane to the analysis of the middle classes.

The whole of Dahrendorf's book is really a dialogue with Marx, chiefly involving a rejection of many of Marx's positions, but also accepting some of the most important, including the thesis of the inevitability of class conflict. Marx's analysis of the class structure is rejected because it is no longer applicable to contemporary society; this has changed in a number of respects, including the increasing heterogeneity ('decomposition') of the bourgeoisie and the proletariat, and the appearance of the middle class (also see Dahrendorf, 1967). Most important, however, Marx was incorrect in his view of property as the basis of social class. The divorce between ownership and control means that any division of society into non-owners and owners is meaningless. In suggesting that property no longer has the sociological function ascribed to it by Marx, Dahrendorf appears to be adopting a position similar to that of Mills. Mills argues, however, that property continues to lie at the base of class in that the authority carried by managers (those who have actual control in the enterprise) derives from the property rights of shareholders, the ultimate owners. Dahrendorf draws almost the opposite conclusion. For him, it is authority that is the more general category from which property rights can be derived. Authority refers to a type of social relation 'independent of economic conditions'. Thus 'the authority structure of entire societies as well as particular institutional orders within societies (such as industry) is, in terms of the theory here advanced, the structural determinant of class formation and class conflict' (Dahrendorf, 1959, p. 136). Those who possess authority form one class, and those without it the other. Authority is, therefore, a dichotomous property, inevitably generating two classes, a point on which Dahrendorf is most insistent. The primary locus of authority is not society at large, for Dahrendorf follows Weber in arguing that authority is primarily exercised in 'imperatively co-ordinated associations' of which the industrial enterprise is the most important example.

The principal argument in Dahrendorf's book is that classes are founded in authority relations, not economic relations: 'it seemed advisable to state, in the strongest possible terms, the way in which class is independent of property, economic conditions, and social stratification' (p. 140). In this rejection of the economic basis of class, Dahrendorf is not 'Weberian' in the sense described by the Incompatibility Thesis, although, ironically, his arguments concerning authority are partly drawn from Weber. Indeed, he quite explicitly rejects occupation (and access to the market) as the basis of class. Occupational differences may generate a form of status stratification, in that differences in income flowing from different occupations will provide varying opportunities for consumption and hence prestige; although, in Dahrendorf's opinion, less so than formerly. Status stratification based on occupation is a form of inequality which may influence the pattern of conflict. It cannot, however, be nearly as important as the division founded on class differences.

There are a number of problems in Dahrendorf's analysis. For example, it is not clear how social classes, based on differences in authority within imperatively co-ordinated associations are constituted in the wider society, beyond the relatively narrow confines of such associations. Again, and perhaps more fundamentally, it might be asked why differences in authority should generate conflict if not by excluding people from the command of economic resources. However, from our point of view, the most significant difficulty confronting Dahrendorf is the Boundary Problem. Unlike many writers in the field, he does see this as a problem. That is, he objects to theories of stratification, theories which see the class structure of modern societies as a continuously graded hierarchy, not composed of discrete classes with well-defined boundaries. As we have seen, Dahrendorf's solution to the Boundary Problem is to argue that there are two social classes with boundaries defined by the possession of, or exclusion from, authority. However, Dahrendorf's arguments for the dichotomous nature of authority, and hence of the class structure, are not convincing. It might be plausible to argue that in any particular situation the authority relationship between two actors is dichotomous. It is not nearly so plausible to suggest that the same will be true of a multiplicity of actors with varying degrees of authority in an enterprise, or between actors who may occupy positions carrying different degrees of authority in a number of imperatively co-ordinated associations (see also Giddens, 1973, p. 73). Dahrendorf does not successfully counter the argument that differences in authority must produce a differentiated class structure rather than a dichotomous one.

The difficulties in Dahrendorf's brave, but extreme, solution to the Boundary Problem show up well in his treatment of the 'New Middle Class'. His theory forces him to allocate various sectors of the middle class to either the bourgeoisie or proletariat, creating difficulties of categorisation rather like those faced by Poulantzas (see Chapter 5 below). Properly speaking, therefore, there is no middle class. It should be noted that this is not due to any process of proletarianisation. There have always been, and will always be, only two classes. In common with many other 'Weberian' writers, Dahrendorf emphasises the heterogeneity of condition of the middle class which was 'born decomposed' and steadily resists the adequate definition of its upper and lower limits. It does not, however, resist being split into two, for Dahrendorf argues that there is a clear division between 'salaried employees who occupy positions that are part of a bureaucratic hierarchy and salaried employees in positions that are not' (p. 55). The former, possessing authority, can be allocated to the superordinate class, and the latter to the subordinate class.

The allocation of middle-class occupations to one or other of two classes is not, however, particularly straightforward in practice. Certain grades of white-collar workers may indeed share the proletarian condition of exclusion from authority. However the position of 'the so-called "staff" of the enterprise, the engineers, chemists, physicists, lawyers, psychologists, and other specialists whose services have become an indispensable part of production in modern firms' (p. 255) is less clear. These categories neither possess authority nor lack it; they are 'beyond the authority structure'. Dahrendorf appears similarly uneasy in identifying the position of bureaucrats who are, as a category, formally assigned to the superordinate class. Bureaucrats are defined very widely as including anybody whose position 'places them on a step of the ladder of administrative jobs' (p. 295). However, it is clear that bureaucracies are differentiated in the degrees of authority possessed by their members and, furthermore, it is very difficult to decide where bureaucracies begin and end (see the discussion of the service class in Chapter 3 below). The Boundary Problem reappears, for how is one to create boundaries round classes in a differentiated population? Dahrendorf does not evade these difficulties by arguing that, because there are no lines of conflict within bureaucracies, they must be in one class or another. Indeed, he rather seems to compound them by appearing to suggest that bureaucracies are relatively insulated: 'they always *belong* to the ruling class but as such never *are* the ruling class' (p. 301); original emphasis).

LOCKWOOD AND THE BLACKCOATED WORKER

The work of Lockwood, and that of Giddens which we discuss next, are well known and we shall restrict our brief discussion to certain of the more fundamental points.

Lockwood's aim is to explain the class-consciousness of clerks, which he takes to be indicated by the relationship of the blackcoated worker to the trade union movement. He points out that the differences between the consciousness of non-manual and manual workers cannot lie in their common class membership. Accordingly, he rejects the notion that clerks and manual workers are both propertyless and therefore in the same class. On the contrary, the explanation of differences in class-consciousness lies in differences in the class position of clerks and manual workers.

Lockwood defines class in terms of three factors: market situation, 'consisting of source and size of income, degree of job-security, and opportunity for upward occupational mobility'; work situation, or 'the set of social relationships in which the individual is involved at work by virtue of his position in the division of labour'; and status situation, or the position in the hierarchy of prestige (1958, p. 12). Actually, Lockwood is not always perfectly consistent in his usage, for at various points in his book he appears to separate status situation from class situation. In any event, he aims to show how the blackcoated worker occupies a different class situation, in his sense, from the manual worker, by considering each dimension of class situation in turn.

As far as market situation is concerned, there has been a narrowing of differentials in respect of wage rates and actual incomes between the two groups. In respect of the conditions of work, job security, pension schemes and opportunities of advancement, clerks continue generally to be rather better off than manual workers. The differences in work situation are more clear-cut, for office employment continues to be organised more around personal and particular social relationships than does the typical factory. There are several reasons for this. Blackcoated work is characteristically organised in small units, resulting in close contacts between workers and management. There are no universally accepted criteria for the standardisation of clerical skills, and consequently each office worker occupies a particular, and often unique, position in the division of work tasks in the office. Lastly, mechanisation of clerical work has had relatively little effect in the rationalisation of the work situation. In the earlier part of the century Lockwood is sure that there were well-marked status differences between clerks and manual workers. However, these have declined under the impact of univeral literacy, the recruitment of clerks from lower social strata and the feminisation of clerical labour. None the less, status differences do persist, even if people are increasingly uncertain of how to apply them, and this 'status ambiguity' is one of the most important obstacles to a common class-consciousness.

In sum: 'As soon as the term "class situation" is understood to cover not only market situation but also work situation, it is clear that clerk and manual worker do not, in most cases, share the same class situation at all' (p. 280). Of the three (or two) elements of class, work situation is the most important. This means that the class differences between blackcoated and manual workers may well be eroded as clerical tasks become mechanised. Indeed, Lockwood hints that such a process of proletarianisation is possible, although it certainly had not happened at the time when he wrote. It is clear, therefore, that Lockwood's definition of the class position of the blackcoated worker is a fluid one: if the work situation changes, then so does the class situation. If class positions differ, then so does class-consciousness. Furthermore, by identifying differences within the class situation of various categories of blackcoated workers, one can explain differences in clerical class-consiousness. Lockwood finds, for example, that differences in the militancy of white-collar unions can best be explained by reference to differences in the work situation of different clerical occupations.

In a sense, Lockwood uses an occupational scheme to show that the class situations of clerical and manual occupations are different and, hence, so is their class-consciousness. What he does not show is the position of these two sets of occupations in the overall class structure of society. He appears, for example, carefully to avoid saying that clerks are middle class. As a result we might suppose that there are a very large number of class situations defined by small differences in market, work and status situations. We are given no theory which would demonstrate how occupational groupings are unified in social classes. However, it is certainly possible that Lockwood would not accept this version of the Boundary Problem as a *problem*. It would be consistent with his method to argue that the definition of class should be adopted which is useful in the 'explanation of particular and concrete events'. Thus, it might be argued that, for certain analytical purposes, class should be defined in terms of a particular collection of market, work and status situations, generating a large number of possible class situations; while, for other tasks, a more general definition should be used, perhaps producing a two- or three-class structure. The employment of the term class to cover all these possibilities might be confusing but nevertheless consistent with a particular 'conventionalist' view of the relationship between sociological concepts and social phenomena.

GIDDENS ON THE MIDDLE CLASS

If Lockwood is concerned with the smaller issue of showing that clerks and manual workers do not occupy the same class situation, but avoids the wider consideration of exploring the class structure as a whole, the same cannot be said of Giddens (1973; also see Giddens, 1980, for a much less Weberian analysis). Like many of the other writers under review, Giddens starts from a consideration of the contrast between Weber and Marx. He does not, however, simply suggest that Weber provides a theory of class better adapted to contemporary society. Indeed, if anything he often seems generally more sympathetic to Marx, although he rejects the labour theory of value which is the centre-piece of Marx's theory of class. Furthermore, in judiciously stating the rival claims of Weber and Marx, Giddens is also careful to point out the similarities between the two writers, for Weber clearly argues that the possession and non-possession of property are the basic categories of class position. 'Indeed, it is easy to exaggerate the degree to which Weber's view departs from that of Marx, especially since, in broadening the concept of "market situation", Weber's argument could be expressed by saying that marketable skills constitute a form of "property" which the individual is able to dispose of to secure a given economic return' (Giddens, 1973, p. 78).

None the less, in the terms set by the Incompatibility Thesis, Giddens is Weberian in his emphasis on market capacity as the crucial determinant of class position and Weberian also in his view that the chief factor influencing market capacity is the possession or non-possession of recognised skills. There are three sorts of market capacity which are important: 'Ownership of property in the means of production; possession of educational or technical qualifications; and possession of manual labour-power'

(p. 107). These three sets of market capacities form the basis of the three-class system that is characteristic of capitalist society. However, the identification of market capacities does not completely provide a map of the class structure of any particular capitalist society, since market capacities vary infinitely and do not automatically create discrete classes with defined boundaries. In effect, Giddens suggests that Weber's scheme involves a similar Boundary Problem for it does not show how the potentially very large variety of class positions can be reduced to a limited number of classes. 'There would appear to be as many "classes", and as many "class conflicts", as there are differing market positions' (p. 104). There therefore has to be some method of making the theoretical transition from the variety of positions carrying different market capacities to classes as 'structured forms'. For Giddens, this transition is effected by the concept of structuration.

There are, then, a number of sources of structuration which intervene between market capacities and social classes. Giddens distinguishes mediate from proximate structurations. The former refers to the distribution of mobility chances in a society. Generally, the more open mobility chances are, the less clearly demarcated classes will be, for mobility makes any homogenisation of experience within a class less likely. There are three sources of proximate structuration: the division of labour within the enterprise, the authority relationships within the enterprise, and the influence of 'distributive groupings', by which Giddens means those groups created by neighbourhood segregation and enjoying a common way of life. The combination of mediate and proximate structuration produces a class structure based on market capacity. In capitalist societies, they systematically generate a three-class structure, although the precise manner in which classes are so structured, and the degree to which they are structured, will vary considerably from one capitalist society to another. The Boundary Problem obtrudes again at this point for it is not clear why 'a threefold class structure is generic to capitalist society' (p. 110). We are not given any reason, in principle, to suppose that the mediate and proximate structurations will necessarily work in this way rather than create a multiplicity of classes out of differences in market capacity.

The analysis of the middle class makes an apt illustration of Giddens's theory. He argues, for example, that dichotomous theories of class (including that of Dahrendorf) must all necessarily fail because they cannot recognise a middle class. The market capacity of middle-class occupations is conferred by educational and technical qualifications. This market capacity produces economic differences of various kinds between white-collar and manual workers. The former have, for example, better earnings and fringe benefits, and better job security. The class position based on this market capacity is structured by mediate and proximate factors. Giddens argues that most mobility studies show that mobility tends to be relatively short-range. There is a buffer-zone between the middle and working classes within which most mobility occurs, and which therefore serves to keep the classes apart. Proximate structurations, it will be remembered, consist of positions within the division of labour, authority relations and 'distributive groupings'. Giddens follows Lockwood in emphasising the well-marked differences between manual and white-collar workers, both in the tasks allocated to them, and in the authority relations within the enterprise. Office work involves little contact with the shop floor, being usually physically quite separate. Communication between the two groups is usually via the foremen. Although management in most enterprises is hierarchical, and white-collar workers are subject to that hierarchy, manual workers, as a group, confront management. Clerks, in other words, participate in the delegation of authority, while manual workers do not. Neighbourhood segregation further reinforces class differences, a factor partly produced by the access to mortgage funds given to white-collar workers by their greater job security and higher overall earnings.

Giddens therefore argues that there are well-defined class differences between manual and white-collar workers. Interestingly, he also suggests that there is no tendency for the automation and mechanisation of office tasks to erode these differences. In his view office mechanisation does not totally transform the labour process as the introduction of machines into factory production transforms manual work. Office machines are adjuncts to clerical labour, not substitutes for it. Automation by the introduction of computers, for example, may reorganise office work. However, this does not result in the proletarianisation of middle-class occupations, since the evidence suggests that computerisation tends to replace routine workers and to increase the demand for skilled personnel. Giddens does not adduce much evidence for this view of the impact of office mechanisation and we shall suggest later that the market and work situations of routine office workers are significantly altered by this process. Giddens further argues that there are no good grounds for supposing that changes in the 'consciousness' of white-collar workers reflect any process of proletarianisation. The middle-class image of society is of a hierarchical arrangement of occupations up which the individuals can move by virtue of their effort – not an image shared by manual workers. Similarly white-collar unionisation, where it exists, does not imply any alliance with working-class trade unions. Therefore,

A class is not a 'group'; the concept, as I have defined it, refers to a cluster of forms of structuration based upon commonly shared levels of market capacity. This applies with particular force to the position of the middle class within the contemporary capitalist societies, since middle class individuals normally lack a clear conception of class indentity and, even when unionised, characteristically do not embrace any form of conflict consciousness. (p. 192).

Although the middle class, as part of a threefold class structure generic to capitalist society, is a given, Giddens is careful to stress that its nature, and the relationships between it and other classes, will necessarily vary from society to society, depending on the particular way that the process of structuration works.

There are considerable difficulties in accepting Giddens's view of the middle class as a large, relatively significant and non-proletarianised entity. Most important, it is difficult to see how all members of the middle class share the market capacity of educational and technical qualifications. It is quite clear that many routine office workers do not have particularly higher qualifications of this kind than many manual workers. It may have been once true that office workers did have a skill – literacy – which commanded a premium, but that is hardly so now. Furthermore, many white-collar jobs do not demand educational or technical qualifications, and there may be a systematic mismatch between the credentials possessed by white-collar workers and the skills required for their work (see Dore, 1976, on the diploma disease). We do not want to argue that credentials are irrelevant to the determination of the middle class (see Chapter 7 below) but only that they do not apply as widely as Giddens would like. Such a conclusion is supported by our earlier contention that Giddens does not take proletarianisation arguments as seriously as they deserve, a point to which we shall return in the next chapter. Lastly, although Giddens is clear on the criteria that theoretically identify the middle class, he is less precise when dealing with empirical materials, as when, for example, he tries to establish the size of the class. Thus discussions of the size of the middle class in various countries are couched in terms of 'non-manual' and 'white-collar' occupations. What is not clear is how these categories match the possession of educational and technical qualifications.

Giddens does concede that although the middle class is conceived of as a unitary class, there are differentiations within it. These can be produced either by differences in market capacity, as in the case of the professions, or by differences in the task performed, as in the differences between, say, managers and secretaries. However, while acknowledging that the class structure of contemporary capitalist societies may seem very fragmented, and class boundaries never precise, Giddens insists that they do follow the threefold pattern. In rejecting Marxist theories and acknowledging fragmentation, yet proposing a fairly strong solution to the Boundary Problem, Giddens shares a position with Dahrendorf. There are similar drawbacks also, for it is not altogether clear, as we have shown, why capitalism must generate a threefold structure and why one should not accept that the class is genuinely more fragmented. In Giddens's case the answer may well lie in the use to which he wishes to put the concept of class for, in rejecting Weber's account, he says that Weber does not show how the variety of class positions is to be reduced to a number of classes 'manageable enough for the explication of major components of social structure and processes of social change' (p. 101). In other words, the analyst adopts a model of the class structure which proves useful in explaining certain features of social reality. We shall return to this point in the next chapter. If Dahrendorf and Giddens are radical in their solution to the Boundary Problem, there are other Weberians who take the heterogeneity of the class structure more seriously. The next text to be considered is a good example of this tendency.

ROBERTS *ET AL.* ON THE FRAGMENTARY CLASS STRUCTURE

The primary concern of Roberts and his co-authors (1977) is not with the 'objective' determinants of class but rather with the images that people form of the class structure and of their place within it. This decision to concentrate on class images is associated with giving subjective elements more theoretical importance than they are credited with by most work in the field. Thus Roberts, Cook, Clark and Semeonoff think that the relationship between objective and subjective factors is of critical sociological moment and, more significantly, that the investigation of class imagery can be fruitful in elucidating broad questions of social change. Even more radically, they appear to find research into objective factors fraught with conceptual difficulty. Thus several 'objective' descriptions of any aspect of social reality are possible, depending on the perspective from which it is approached. 'The one certainty is that to treat the subject we must adopt some method of categorisation, otherwise we are unable to handle the evidence. What we cannot do is to assume that one preferred method of categorisation enjoys a unique affinity with objective reality' (p. 4). Now, it is not clear that this problem of objectivity utilises the concept in the same way as in the contrast between objective determinants of class and subjective class images. It is, after all, possible to have rival 'objective' interpretations of the 'subjective' data of class imagery. However, Roberts *et al.* do convey the impression that research on class imagery is not a mere adjunct to the work on class determination, and that subjective perceptions of class situation are critical for any understanding of the class structure.

Roberts *et al.* suggest that arguments about class are often simply arguments about definitions and definitions cannot be either right or wrong. They say:

> We are employing stratification as a general term to refer to the processes of interplay between the variables involved in systems of inequality. Differences in wealth, income, and other factors that individuals order hierarchically are referred to as inequalities, the structures of which can be ascertained independently of individuals' subjective assessments. Aggregates of individuals located at particular points in such systems

of inequalities are called strata. Classes are defined as the collectivities with which individuals identify themselves in making the hierarchical environments they inhabit meaningful. (p. 18)

In terms of both stratum and class, the distinction between manual and white-collar workers or, more generally, between working and middle class is a meaningful one. Thus, white-collar workers are better paid, have better career earnings, higher chances of promotion (particularly if they are men), more extensive fringe benefits of all kinds and better access to consumption goods like housing. As far as class images are concerned, the distinction between middle and working class is well understood by respondents and, what is more, the capacity for making the distinction is highly correlated with the respondent's own self-perception as middle or working class, and voting behaviour and trade union membership.

Roberts *et al.* therefore argue that the middle-class/working-class, manual/white-collar divide represents a significant break in the class structure both subjectively and objectively. However, this does not mean that one can treat either class as a unified block. The middle class, especially, is more fragmented than unitary, showing far greate disparities of conditions within it than the working class. Indeed, in their sense of the term it is difficult to speak of it as a class at all. It may once have been unified, in the sense of being a class of self-employed entrepreneurs, but changes in the economy have diversified white-collar occupations. This is not to say that the 'old' middle class no longer exists. Roberts *et al.* identify the self-employed as a first distinct fragment of the middle class that may well continue to carry political power in local authorities. This group felt threatened by the working class, while feeling that they gained no support from their economic equals or betters. They tended to describe the middle class as a compressed and small group squeezed between a large working class and a powerful upper class. Although generally they were more right wing than other middle-class groups, their politics were an apparently odd mixture of solid Conservative opinions and radical views. A large minority, for example, favoured the extension of public ownership.

As for the second fragment, the most common type of class imagery found in white-collar respondents involved individuals placing themselves in a large middle class – a 'middle mass', which often included manual workers. These respondents tended to have incomes clustered around the average for the white-collar group as a whole. They have attitudes conventionally regarded as characteristic of the middle class, being Conservative, opposing further public ownership and considering that trade unions are becoming too powerful (although there was a fairly large union membership among this group).

The third fragment of the middle class discovered by Roberts *et al.* is that of white-collar proletarians. This group placed themselves in the same class as manual workers and saw a sharp division between them and something they called the middle class. They typically had relatively low incomes and minimal education. They manifested less 'conservative' views than other sections of the white-collar groups and were more likely to belong to trade unions. 'Their outlook was "working class" in the full sense of the term' (p. 140).

The fourth and last fragment is chiefly distinguished by its relatively high educational attainment in full-time higher education. Its members are well paid, well satisfied with their jobs and geographically mobile. They manifested a particular kind of intellectual radicalism. That is, they were a great deal more radical than other white-collar workers on such 'liberal' issues as race relations, capital punishment, or the 'crime problem'. The contrast on other matters was not quite so marked, but the more highly educated were less likely to have voted Conservative and less likely to complain that the trade unions are too powerful.

There are therefore four principal white-collar images of society which generally vary with the individual's position in the white-collar hierarchy. Thus, an awareness of belonging to a middle mass is characteristic of those 'comfortably positioned around the middle' of the white-collar hierarchy. Proletarian consciousness is restricted to those at the bottom of the hierarchy, engaged in routine occupations with low pay. Roberts *et al.* are careful to note that proletarian awareness is generated by middle-class processes, for the critical issue seems to be that those at the bottom of the hierarchy are being denied rewards which can only be achieved by collective action. The middle class is therefore being splintered and is likely to become more so. The growth of large-scale organisations generates a lot of secure and relatively well paid jobs restricting 'career opportunities, authority, and demanding work to the qualified; thereby leaving a white collar proletariat to discharge routine functions in offices, laboratories and workshops, while, simultaneously, this same trend threatens members of the middle class who have earned their status in traditional ways – by entering a family business or by working their ways into senior positions by loyal and diligent service' (p. 143). The view of the *new* middle class (as distinct from the self-employed) is therefore of a number of fragments being progressively driven apart, with one section (14 per cent in this study) becoming proletarianised.

It is not, however, altogether clear how one is to interpret this view of the fragmentation of the middle class, a difficulty raised by the authors' distinction between subjective and objective conceptions of class. Are we to assume, since this is a study of class images, that fragmentation refers only to the perceptions of respondents, or also to the 'objective' situation of middle-class occupations? This problem is not clarified by the authors' distinction between class and stratum discussed earlier. Strata are aggregates of individuals located at particular points in a system of inequality, defined independently of respondents' perceptions. Classes, on the other hand, are those collectivities with which individuals identify themselves. Unfortunately, as we have indicated, Roberts *et al.* do not always distinguish these in their discussion. In their account, for example, of the way that the 'old' middle class has given way to a new middle class, we are not told whether this represents the decay of the homogeneity of perception or condition.

We are, therefore, left uncertain about the basis for the fragmentation of the middle class. Lack of resolution in this respect is related to another difficulty – a more familiar one – created by Roberts *et al.*'s conceptual scheme. Thus, strata are defined as collections of individuals located at points in the system of unequal distributions of rewards. Again, such a formulation raises the Boundary Problem in that no method is given for creating out of the continuously graded hierarchy of inequalities a set of those entities that other writers call classes. It may well be that this is not a difficulty that Roberts *et al.* take very seriously and that they intend to give greater theoretical weight to what *they* call classes. Thus they could argue, and this is perhaps implied in their choice of terms, that there are no such things as classes in the 'objective' sense and that strata only become meaningfully organised into larger aggregates by individuals' perceptions that those aggregates exist. There are a number of objections to such a view, the most important of which is that individuals' class imagery is not arbitrary and is, in part, produced by the structure of 'objectively' determined classes. There is an alternative possibility for the organisation of strata, one which is also implied at times by Roberts *et al.* Strata could be aggregated as statistical entities, that is, as clusters in the distribution of inequality. This possibility can also be criticised, for it appears sociologically arbitrary, especially if individuals are distributed along more than one dimension of inequality.

3

Themes in Weberian Analysis

The last chapter has shown, among other things, that there is considerable diversity among Weberians. If there is a discrete body of Weberian theory, it may be constituted by its distinctive treatment of a number of different themes rather than by its sole emphasis on the market. We now continue our examination of various theories of the middle class by considering the manner in which the Weberian literature deals with certain matters that must be critical in any analysis of the middle class. Of necessity, our discussion must be selective, raising issues which will be treated again in Part Two.

THE SIZE AND SIGNIFICANCE OF THE MIDDLE CLASS

The claim that there are occupational groupings, however vaguely defined, between the working class and the bourgeoisie is clearly a major issue in contemporary writings on modern society. None the less, there is still considerable debate about the nature and importance of this intermediate element. In particular there is no clear agreement as to the size or the significance of the middle class.

In much of the sociological literature on class, the distinction between manual and non-manual occupations is assigned considerable importance. Very often this distinction is used to make aggregate comparisons between the two groups, as when Goldthorpe *et al.* (1969) investigated the affluent working class. Sometimes, however, the term 'non-manual' is used to stand for the 'middle class'. More specifically, Giddens argues, as we have seen, that there is a middle class based on a market capacity, namely, educational and technical qualifications. Giddens does not make clear the limits of this class or its size, and the statistics that he gives (29 per cent of the workforce in 1959) again refer to non-manual occupations. It would appear that he uses the terms 'non-manual', 'white collar' and 'new middle class' more or less interchangeably, not a procedure which would make it easy to use a criterion like 'educational and technical qualifications' to delimit the size of the middle class. For one thing, such a criterion might be taken to rule out a large number of routine white-collar workers. Giddens recognises that this group does constitute a distinctive fraction of the middle class, but he still argues that they are not proletarianised. Despite these considerable difficulties of interpretation, Giddens gives the impression that the middle class represents a sizeable proportion of the employed population.

The notion of the 'service class' also represents the view that there is an intermediate grouping which has considerable social significance. This idea made its first appearance in the work of Renner (1953, first English translation). He argues that as capitalism develops and increases in the scale of its operations, the capitalist increasingly employs people to carry out the functions that he can no longer perform personally. The capitalist delegates his functions to employees who perform these services for him. This service class is not only employed in private business. It also makes its appearance in public bodies, there performing services for capital of a rather more indirect kind. It is important for Renner that service workers are not wage workers and he feels that the fact that they are salaried represents an important difference. They do not produce commodities but rather 'dispose of the values that have been produced' (p. 249). The service class is therefore separated both from the bourgeoisie and from the working class, a separation reinforced in the latter case by the caste-like qualities of the service class. The fact that the service class cannot be identified with the propertyless now does not, however, mean that this will always be the case. Indeed, Renner detects some changes in the situation of the service class. Its inherited property has become less significant, its life-style is becoming more like that of the working class, and nationalisation of private enterprise has 'established a bridge between the public services and private employment, between the situation of the worker, and that of the employee' (pp. 250–1).

Renner's conception of the service class has been adopted by other writers, although often with considerable modification. Croner (1954; and Bain and Price, 1972), for example, proposes a functional definition of the salaried worker as having supervisory, planning, administrative and commercial functions. The explanation of the separate and special position of salaried workers in modern societies 'lies in the fact that their duties were once performed by the employer', the four functions being originally 'subdivisions of the general responsibility assumed by the employer' (p. 105). This delegation of responsibility has evolved historically in five stages. First, the employer himself takes on all five functions. Secondly, over time, some of these functions become diffused into the employer's family. In the third stage, outsiders are brought in to act as special assistants to the employer, with the prospect of becoming heads of businesses themselves. Eventually the duties of these executives become subdivided into specialised jobs and occupations, particularly those of foremen. Lastly, the increasing division of labour of the entrepreneurial function produces a shift away from the workshop and the foreman to the dominance of the administrative staff.

Dahrendorf (1969) also employs the concept of a service class, retaining the idea of delegation but, instead of seeing the services as being performed for the capitalist, locating them in the context of bureaucracy. The members of the service class are bureaucrats whose main function is the administration of laws, thereby acting as a bridge between the rulers and the ruled. Dahrendorf admits that bureaucrats differ a good deal from one another, especially in that there may be a large gap between those at the top of the ladder and those at the bottom. However, despite these differences Dahrendorf still insists that bureaucrats should be considered together as the service class, since they are all on a bureaucratic ladder together whatever their relative positions.

The *term* 'service class' has more recently been used in the investigation of social mobility carried out by Goldthorpe and his colleagues (1980b). In this study the authors construct a social class schema in which there are seven classes. The first of these, representing 14 per cent of the working population, comprises 'all higher-grade professionals, self-employed or salaried; higher-grade administrators and officials in central and local government and in public and private enterprises (including company directors); managers in large industrial establishments; and large proprietors' (p. 39). This class includes, according to Goldthorpe, what Dahrendorf says is the upper part of his service class plus independent businessmen and 'free' professionals (although a different definition is adopted later in the study). However, in two directions Goldthorpe's notion of the service class departs from earlier conceptions. First, it is an aggregation of occupations rather than a class united by the performance of services for a capitalist or within a bureaucracy. Secondly, it is not an intermediate class but is rather at the top of the hierarchy. The idea that the service class is in some sense a middle class is critical in the views of Renner and Dahrendorf.

The concept of service class is, therefore, distinctly slippery. In its 'classical' formulations (rather than in Goldthorpe's treatment) it represents an intermediate grouping, small (Dahrendorf puts it at 12 per cent of the employed population), but with some social significance. It is hard to say how much significance it has, for Renner speaks of its impending proletarianisation, while Dahrendorf says that, despite its title, the service class is not really a class, but is rather an aggregation of ruling groups.

The use of the term 'intermediate class' also diminishes the significance of the middle class. For example, for Westergaard and Resler (1975) the major cleavage in society is between the propertied and the non-propertied. Possession of property remains the crucial source of wealth and the main cause of inequality in income. For example, Westergaard and Resler record the estimate that five-sixths of income units have no investment income at all, while 10 per cent have two-thirds of the total, 5 per cent three-fifths of it, and 1 per cent over a third. Furthermore, inequality in general is only a composite of inequality on several dimensions. Thus, the dominant position of the propertied is based on their holdings of property and the income they derive from it, but also on their ability to command well-paid jobs, their capacity to provide, and benefit from, advantageous educational provision, and their political power.

The propertied represent the major group at the top but Westergaard and Resler believe that there are other groups sufficiently similar that they should be added. Thus, of those individuals who have to work by selling their labour-power, a small group of directors, managers, established professionals and high officials can be separated from the rest. They do not have a great deal in common with other salary-earners. Senior business executives, for example, can more or less set their own pay, and established professionals have a great deal of control, through their professional associations, over their rewards.

These two categories of individuals, comprising 5 – 10 per cent in all, represent the tiny privileged elite. The remainder are entirely dependent on the sale of their labour. The cleavage between the elite and the mass is the crucial one and is the principal line along which actual or potential class conflict forms, a conclusion emphasised by calling this group a ruling interest in its use of political power. Indeed, Westergaard and Resler are reluctant to concede that there are any significant cleavages within the mass of workers dependent on the labour market. They dislike the term 'middle class' because it obscures the important differences within that group. For the same reason, the distinction between manual and non-manual employments is criticised because it places too diverse a set of individuals into the non-manual category. The important point is that the terms 'middle class' and 'non-manual work' serve to conceal the important propertied/non-propertied distinction. The middle class, as conventionally conceived, consists of both propertied and non-propertied elements which should properly be separated. We have already seen how the most privileged sections of managers, professionals and officials should be allocated to the 'propertied' group. Westergaard and Resler also take the view that a very large sector of the middle class shares so much of the inequality of condition of the manual working class that they all belong in the same category. In other words, they hold the view that the middle class, or certain sections of it, are proletarianised. In terms of earnings and income over the life-cycle there is very little to choose between white-collar and manual work. It is true that in certain other respects there are differences. White-collar workers have shorter hours, greater security of employment, better fringe benefits and wider opportunities for promotion. But these advantages are being diminished, mostly through the advance of manual workers. 'By criteria relating to material conditions, power, and individual opportunity, low-grade office workers and the like are partly within the "working class", partly on its fringes; not distinctively outside it, as conventional usage still implies' (p. 349).

It is noteworthy that the analysis of the conditions of routine white-collar workers is similar to that of Lockwood but the conclusions drawn from it are very different. While Lockwood uses his evidence to emphasise the continuing differences between white-collar and manual work, Westergaard and Resler use theirs to stress the similarities. The latter argues that, considered as a group, routine white-collar workers and manual workers represent some three-quarters of the employed population. This leaves an 'intermediate group', comprising 15–20 per cent, between the elite and the mass. This group is made up of such occupations as junior and middle management in public and private industry, technical staff and 'lower-tier professions' such as teachers, social workers and nurses. These occupations have definite advantages over the condition of the manual and routine white-collar worker despite the fact that they too have to sell their labour. Their incomes are higher and they have increasing earnings as they get older. They enjoy considerable fringe benefits and more relaxed conditions of work. As a result their lives have a certain 'security, predictability and opportunity for individual investment in the future'. However, despite these advantages, this group is marginal, for it still depends on the sale of labour. Furthermore, Westergaard and Resler argue that a large element, the 'lower professions', have suffered a relative erosion of income rather like that of clerks.

At one point Westergaard and Resler refer, grudgingly, to this intermediate group as a middle class. More often, however, they suggest that it is a fragmented, sometimes insecure, rough grouping whose members do not have a great deal in common. The major, dominant, cleavage in capitalist societies, between the propertied and the non-propertied, leaves no space for a middle class, only for a few fragments, a straggling set of occupational groupings.

A similar conception of the middle class as a kind of asteroidal belt between two planets, perhaps of some size but of limited significance, is automatically produced, as we have seen, by dichotomous theories like that of Dahrendorf (see also Parkin, 1972). In a relatively early statement Cole (1950) sums up the view that the middle class is not a real class by saying that the term 'tends to become a merely descriptive adjective, designating those in the middle, rather than a term defining a distinctive section of the population' (p. 290).

In conclusion, much of the literature argues that there is some grouping 'in the middle'. However, there is generally no clear conviction of the significance of this grouping. Its size is often not specified and there are some doubts as to whether it is a *class* at all. Certainly it has no unity in the conventional sense, of consciousness, action, or even structure. Further, as we shall show later, many authors favour some version of a proletarianisation thesis which further reduces the importance of intermediate groupings.

COMPLEXITY AND FRAGMENTATION

One of the features that might make the middle class a less cohesive force is its diversified and fragmented nature. Benson (1978), for example, draws attention 'to the difficulty of speaking of *the* middle class, except in the context of comparisons with the working class. The non-manual stratum is differentiated to an extent not really matched by the ranks of manual labour' (p. 107). King and Raynor (1981) conclude a recent survey of sociological work on the middle class by saying that 'while the middle class has never comprised a coherent unity, even in the classic bourgeois age of the nineteenth century, it is even more of a heterogeneous grouping today' (p. 242). Bechhofer *et al.* (1978) argue that the middle class is more differentiated and heterogeneous both occupationally and culturally than it once was:

> the 'middle class' in Britain today is a less established, less unified 'middle class'. It contains not only a good many individuals recruited from manual backgrounds . . . but it encompasses a very large number of totally new positions . . . the result is less normative coherence or unity in the ranks of the middle class. In the transformation of the occupational structure there are developments tending to weaken the unity of the middle class, and likely to lead to diverse interests and claims which may be pursued in a variety of ways. (p. 419)

This diversity has been produced by a number of trends. There have been large increases in the Higher Professional and Lower Professional and Technical groups, and the rise in clerical, sales and service workers has been levelling off. Furthermore, there has been a great increase in female employment in routine white-collar occupations and the men in such occupations are either young, and hoping for promotion, or relatively old, having come from manual employment. Sex and age characteristics have therefore made the middle class more heterogeneous. Thus Bechhofer *et al.* argue that the occupational changes have created four distinct groupings within the class. First, there is an elite of managers, top executives and consultants. Secondly, small businessmen form a group under pressure both from large businesses and from the state. Thirdly, there are professionals, under even greater pressure from the state, progressively losing their independence and being drawn into bureaucracies. Fourthly, there is a relatively large group of routine clerical, administrative and technical workers, becoming proletarianised, losing any authority that they might have had, and with job security very little better than that enjoyed by manual workers.

These conclusions concerning occupational differentiation within the middle class are very much reinforced by the many studies of specific middle-class occupations. The studies of the petty bourgeoisie, particularly of shop-keepers by Bechhofer and his associates (1968, 1974a, 1974b, 1976), for example, show not only the diversity of conditions within the middle class, but also the difficulty of referring to this group as middle class at all. The most striking thing to emerge from this research is the 'marginality' of small shop-keepers, and the authors at one point suggest that they are outside the class structure, although there is good evidence that shop-keepers have always been somewhat marginal (see Crossick, 1977a).

Over the years the market share of small shops has declined but the number of such shops has not. The result is that already low returns per shop are depressed even further. In 1968 many of the small independent traders studied by Bechhofer *et al.* (1968) were earning very little more than many manual workers. This relatively low income was earned by very long hours of work in poor conditions. The average working day was 10½ hours, with the two most numerous groups of traders, grocers and newsagents, exceeding this figure (at between 11 and 12 hours per day). Many of the businesses surveyed kept going by relying on family labour, and owners were often subsidised by income coming into the family from outside or by eroding capital. It is true that owning a shop affords some economic advantages. Thus it seems that small traders own consumer durables and houses to a greater extent than do comparable income groups.

Despite the apparent unattractiveness of the economic situation of small shop-keepers, there is no shortage of recruits. Small traders value independence and working for themselves above all else. This value is reflected in the ways in which they conduct their business. For example, Bechhofer *et al.* point out that small shop-keepers are reluctant to join the large buying organisations run by wholesalers or even associations of small businessmen. Bechhofer *et al.* point out that this determined individualism is surprising given the economic pressure on the small shop-keeper from large retailers.

These features of small traders distinguish them from all other groups in the class structure. The petty bourgeoisie do not properly belong to the middle class, to the bourgeoisie, or to the working class. They have property and are their own masters, yet they have a relatively low income and poor working conditions.

> The small traders really do deserve to be treated as a separate stratum, separate, that is, from both the so-called lower middle class and from skilled and independent manual workers ... in some respects shop-keepers may be regarded as a stratum moulded by the economic forces of another era, and in their attitudes and values, their orientations to work and politics, we find echoes of another age. (Bechhofer *et al.*, 1974b, p. 105)

PROLETARIANISATION

If there is any one issue that dominates the literature on the middle class, it is that of proletarianisation. Clearly, one response to the 'discovery' of the middle class is to argue that the apparent superiority in the life-chances of members of the middle classes is only illusory, and that a substantial section of white-collar workers should properly be included in the working class.

In general, the evidence concerning proletarianisation is not clear-cut. One of the difficulties in assessing the evidence is that there is no obvious agreement as to the criteria by which one is to judge whether or not a particular sector of the middle class has been proletarianised. Most particularly, is one to refer to market conditions, especially wages, or work conditions, or to attitudes and behaviour? In addition, within each of these categories there is a whole series of issues to be confronted. For example, in considering the work situation, one will have to ask whether or not 'deskilling', a heightened division of labour, a reduced area of autonomous decision-making, and absorption into larger bureaucracies, are all equally relevant to the proletarianisation of any group.

Starting with market situation, there is widespread agreement that there is a fairly well-marked gap between average manual and non-manual earnings, a gap, furthermore, which has been remarkably constant over the last seventy years or so. This apparent persistent difference is reinforced by continuing differences in earnings over the career as a whole, fringe benefits of different kinds and job security. Many writers make a good deal of this gap in market conditions, particularly as they attempt to counter popular speculation that the position of the middle class is being eroded (Giddens, 1973). However, aggregate comparisons of this kind are misleading and it is clear that there are substantial overlaps between non-manual and manual occupations if one breaks down the larger categories. Westergaard and Resler (1975), for example, argue that there have been striking changes in the position of two groups, 'lower professions' and 'clerks', whose pay has dropped in relation to other groups. This does not reflect any general trend towards equalisation, for manual workers have not improved their position with respect to the average. It rather represents a proletarianisation of clerks and the lower professions. Furthermore, in examining the earnings of individual occupations in more detail it is clear that clerks and shop assistants are among the lowest paid male workers. Kelly (1980), in his study of civil servants, confirms this view. He found, as have others, that there had been a decline nationally in the manual/non-manual differential and this was reflected in civil service salaries. Management grades, however, had more or less held their own, while among 'clerks a very definite decline in salaries *vis-à-vis* manual workers has occurred and Civil Service clerks have done even less well than clerks in other occupations' (p. 131). Nor have clerks preserved their better situation in their career earnings, which follow a similar pattern to those of manual workers (though see detail and qualifications in Westergaard and Resler, 1975, pp. 80–3). In respect of hours of work, fringe benefits, pension schemes, sick pay schemes and job security, routine white-collar workers may be better placed, although the evidence does not allow very precise discriminations within the non-manual sector. There is some evidence, however, that the traditional resistance of clerical grades to unemployment when compared to manual workers is being eroded (see APEX, 1980; Hill, 1981, ch. 9).

A more subtle way in which the market situation of routine white-collar workers may differ from that of manual workers is in the greater promotion prospects enjoyed by non-manual workers in general. The recent study by Stewart *et al*. (1980) offers data which bear on this question. The authors' starting point is a consideration of the age structure of the occupation 'clerk'. There are two age peaks which seem to represent two distinct elements, ex-manual workers moving into clerical work with advancing age, and those starting as clerks who will mostly move out of the occupation with advancing age. The age distribution of clerks is presumptive evidence that clerical work represents a route of upward mobility. As the authors say:

> The general picture of male clerical employment, then, is of large numbers of young men recruited straight from school or very soon afterwards, who in the earlier years form a large majority of clerks. They then move progressively to other employment, especially during their 20s, and after age 30 form a smaller proportion of clerks than do ex-manual workers. These latter are fairly rare at younger ages, but gradually their numbers increase to a peak between ages 50 and 60. Recruits from other areas of non-manual work are much less common than ex-manual workers. They are in greatest numbers between 20 and 30, falling thereafter to a very small proportion. This is consistent with a view that many of them after moving into this area of employment subsequently move out again as their careers develop. To some extent we would expect that the younger ex-manual workers would follow a similar pattern, that for them entry to clerical work is the route to a more successful white collar career rather than a final resting place. (p. 129)

Further evidence is provided by examining the promotion prospects and histories of clerks. If one takes age 30 as the watershed in a clerical career, after that age current clerks form only 19 per cent of all those starting careers as clerks; that is, 81 per cent of all those who began as clerks and are still in white-collar occupations have been been promoted. As one might expect, promotion prospects vary from industry to industry. Within manufacturing, for example, the pattern of the proportions in promoted positions is unlike other sectors. It starts earlier, rises more sharply than that for insurance and less sharply than that for public service at early ages, but reaches a peak earlier than either. Of course, in considering promotion and mobility one must take into account not only the chances of promotion, but the distance travelled. Stewart *et al*. do believe that promotion is likely to be long-range. If one takes promotion into management as an index of such mobility, an analysis of the origins of managers shows that opportunities to rise into management have not decreased in the postwar era and there has not been a large volume of direct recruitment into management. There has not, furthermore, been any disproportionate rise in the educational experience and attainment of managers.

Stewart *et al.* argue that, because of the way that clerks move over their work life, they cannot be treated as an occupational grouping in the orthodox way.

> We do not assume that we are dealing with 'the clerk' or that he has a 'peculiar social situation'. Those employed in clerical work come to it from diverse backgrounds and social experience, and while some may complete their careers in this type of work, others will leave to a great diversity of occupational careers. The clerk does not have a peculiar social location. To seek the class positions of clerks, as if they were a homogeneous group in their relationship to stratification processes, is to confuse the position (or more correctly, positions) of clerical work in the productive system with the position of those employed in such work in the labour market. In fact the latter has to be separately specified, and clerks are in diverse relationships to the labour market. (p. 191)

Specifically, one cannot therefore talk sensibly about the proletarianisation of clerks. Either young clerks have been promoted, or older clerks coming in from manual work, and women, have always been proletarian. In sum, while there may have been a degradation of work tasks, no people have been proletarianised, therefore there is no proletarianisation.

The argument of Stewart *et al.* that clerical work represents an occupational category through which people pass on their way to management positions is given some support by the data from the Oxford mobility study (Goldthorpe, 1980b; Heath, 1981). However, these recent studies of social mobility are largely based on the mobility experiences of male employees and discussion of white-collar and clerical employment must take account of the obvious fact that these occupations are largely female (for general discussion, see Garnsey, 1978).

One of the most striking features of the white-collar occupations is their feminisation. In 1911, 11 per cent of clerks were women; in 1921, 44 per cent; in 1951, 59 per cent; and in 1971 the proportion had risen to 71 per cent (calculated from Routh, 1980, p. 24). In some occupations the proportion is even higher. Almost 99 per cent of secretaries and 83 per cent of telephone operators, for example, are women (Murgatroyd, 1982). Office employment has, of course, attracted women for some considerable time (Davies, 1974) and women formed the bulk of office labour well before office work became noticeably automated (Rhee, 1968, pp. 25–6). Furthermore, other white-collar employments, such as that of shop assistant, have been female preserves for some time (Woodward, 1960). However, taking white-collar work as a whole, women have not greatly improved their position in the higher reaches, but have come to dominate the more routine work, as Table 1·1 showed. This heavy concentration of women in routine white-collar work is reflected in their lower rates of pay. The New Earnings Survey of 1977, for example, showed that the average hourly pay of adult male clerical workers was 167·1 pence while their female counterparts only earned 129·3 pence (McNally, 1979, p. 46), although there is some evidence that women's average pay is increasing faster than that of men (Routh, 1980). Promotion prospects for women in routine white-collar jobs are also limited, certainly more limited than those for young men in the same occupations, although the available evidence is scarce (Blackburn, 1967; McNally, 1979; Heath, 1981). Of course, the relative lack of female mobility is related to greater mobility of male clerks. Men are permitted greater promotion opportunities as white-collar employments are reorganised and mechanised (Lockwood, 1958). As Crozier (1965) puts it, men 'were pushed toward more skilled occupations and toward executive positions, so that the general proletarianisation of the white-collar group – which seems quite clear if one analyses its composition, its remuneration, and its tasks in the abstract – were not experienced as such by those directly involved' (p. 16).

The market situation of white-collar work is, therefore, clearly dependent on the gender composition of the labour force in these occupations or, more generally, on the role of gender discrimination in the labour market. Whether or not gender has an independent effect is a matter of some debate and, as Murgatroyd (1982) points out, gender may have a role in creating occupations as well as assigning particular kinds of people to those occupations (see also Downing, 1980). A similar point is made by McNally (1979) in stressing the feminine characteristics of certain white-collar occupations. Secretaries, for example, are expected to serve their employer as well as to type. The process of feminisation is also related to the work situation of white-collar employments, for the mechanisation of office work has brought women into these occupations as it has helped to promote men. It is to this question of the impact of office machines on the work situation that we now turn.

Clearly, mechanisation in the office is nothing new (see Rhee, 1968, pp. 36ff.). However, the introduction of the computer does mark a distinctive step and there was a persistent tendency in the earlier literature to underestimate the ability of machines to replace human skills. One of the most important technical effects of the introduction of the computer is the possibility of integrated data-processing. As Rhee argues, the essence of integrated data-processing

is its assumed capability of transforming the dispersed data processing of the separate organizational units and sections into a closed system, designed to integrate completely all the information needs of the *entire* organization. This is to be understood as meaning that all data relevant to a single organization's business can be fed into a *single system* and lead to rational decisions. (p. 56; author's emphasis)

The computer may represent a particularly dramatic way of reorganising office work but other machines have also replaced particular traditional skills. Duplicators, photocopiers, dictating and addressing machines and, more recently, word-processors, have all had a large and growing impact in large offices. Within the period 1956–66 in the civil service there was a 400 per cent increase in the number of dictating machines and a 100 per cent increase in duplicators and photocopiers (Kelly, 1980). Some indication of the extent of office mechanisation can also be gauged from the numbers of persons employed in various branches of office work. Routh (1980), for example, shows that the number of typists increased much faster than the rest of the clerical group between 1931 and 1951. In the next twenty years, however, the number of office machine operators increased rapidly while typists just about kept pace with the group as a whole. There are indications that since 1971 the proportional rate of decline in the typist category has accelerated.

We have already argued that the computer permits an integrated approach to the handling of office work. This also means a centralisation of activities, a tendency also produced by the introduction of other machines. These are all so expensive that it only makes economic sense to have them concentrated in one place, a 'word-processing centre', for example, to benefit from economies of scale. Centralisation of this kind will clearly have implications for the conditions of work of white-collar employees, but it would be misleading to attribute these effects entirely to the machines themselves. It is the way that machines are allied to completely new ways of organising *human* labour that will have the most significant impact on the work situation. Indeed, in the literature designed to help management with the introduction of computers it is constantly emphasised that mere mechanisation is insufficient. Machines are only efficient to the extent that they are incorporated into a reorganised labour process (Mumford and Ward, 1968). Early failures in the use of office automation have been attributed to a mistaken emphasis on hardware and the slow speed of the introduction of word-processors to the inability to reorganise the flow of work (Burns, 1980) – an inability often due to the resistance of both management and workers (Earl, 1980).

It is often argued that automation embedded in changed methods of work produces conditions of work that approximate to those enjoyed or not enjoyed by manual workers. Office work becomes more routine, involves a smaller sphere of decision and responsibility, is more subject to managerial control, involves less skill, and takes place in organisations that are larger, more bureaucratised, and characterised by a minute division of labour. Kelly (1980) puts the argument thus: 'The long-term effect will be to create a new division of labour in the office itself where one lowly group of workers will be employed in routine tasks and will operate the machine whose tasks are rationalised and subdivided, while above them a new group of controllers with specialist knowledge will emerge' (p. 87; for a brief statement see Cooley, 1977). The bulk of the sociological literature does favour some version of the argument that clerical work has been affected in this way. Downing (1980), for example, argues:

> the move to word processing effectively transfers the control which the typist has over a conventional typewriter on to the machine itself. Word processors are designed with supervisory and monitoring elements built into them. In addition, the word processor can perform all the elementary functions of typing which take a person years to perfect. (p. 283).

The introduction of the word-processor thus takes away a substantial degree of control over the typists' work, permits a lower level of skill, fragments the labour process, for example, by having printing done elsewhere, and lessens personal contact between typists, and between typists and principals. McNally (1979) distinguishes the secretary from the routine office worker. Her analysis of the latter is similar to Downing's in that the worker is seen as being machine-paced, performing entirely routine work, and separated from management. However, in her view, even the personal secretary's position is being undermined by office reorganisation, since mechanisation has made typing and shorthand obsolete skills and therefore 'the boss no longer needs a personal secretary, since all the tasks which do not involve shorthand and typing can now be performed by one girl who is employed to keep the diaries of several executives' (p. 72). Mumford and Banks (1967) make the comparison between factory and office explicit:

> The modern office is no longer a small and friendly place. On the contrary, it may be enormous, full of machines and like a factory in its flow of work. The advent of large-scale mechanisation, and in particular the electronic computer, has increased its resemblance to the shop floor and many jobs, usually those performed by women, make demands on the clerk similar to those made on the worker by factory production lines. (p. 22)

The arguments employed here are similar to those suggesting that the manual worker is being progressively deskilled (Braverman, 1974; see Chapter 4 below). The counter-arguments are similar, too.

As we showed in the last chapter, both Lockwood and Giddens argue against a proletarianisation thesis based on the impact of office mechanisation, although they are essentially concerned to stress the continuing differences between the middle and working classes (see also Heritage, 1980). Some authors argue that automation both eliminates the dull, routine jobs and raises the skill level required to operate the new machines. Much of the more management-oriented literature tends to concentrate on the productivity advantages, or the possibilities of better control and more efficient decision-making, from office mechanisation. Incidentally, however, it is sometimes suggested that reorganisation may enlarge the responsibilities of some levels of white-collar work, such as administrative secretaries (EDP Analyzer, 1980). Earl (1980) also suggests that micro-computers provide for some measure of decentralisation in an organisa-tion because they provide independent bases of data provision and analysis. It seems more likely, however, that he is talking of the possibili-ties of relative departmental autonomy rather than the potential indepen-dence of employees from employers. In a more general vein, Kohn (1971) argues against the common view of bureaucracies, suggesting that they actually give greater opportunities for initiative to all workers, whatever their position in the hierarchy.

A great deal of the debate about proletarianisation concentrates on the position of routine white-collar workers. A number of studies (a review is to be found in Rhee, 1968) also suggest that management, particularly middle management, loses particular functions after the reorganisation of the office. The power to make decisions, often offered as the definition of management, passes up the hierarchy to top management or to the new specialist groups. As Mumford and Ward (1968) say of middle manage-ment: 'Many of these men are concerned with routine control procedures, the solution of well structured problems and the supervision of staff. The first two of these functions can be transferred to a computer with ease' (p. 95; see also Earl, 1980). The removal of decision-making powers can be fairly thoroughgoing. Morenco (1965) shows how a computer was used to make decisions that would otherwise have been taken by a bank manager. At the same time, the supervisory functions of middle management will be affected by automation even if they are not replaced. That is, to the extent that routine work lower down the hierarchy is performed by machine and is closely mechanically integrated, the requirement for supervision is cor-respondingly lessened.

STATUS, CONSCIOUSNESS AND ACTION

As we suggested in Chapter 1, the concept of status has been utilised in investigations of the class structure, especially in American work, which often simply assumes that class is equivalent to status (for example, Hatt, 1950) without any argument. The same holds for earlier British studies of stratification in which prestige scales were used as an index of class posi-tion (Hall and Caradog Jones, 1950). A number of books specifically on the middle class drew attention to the differences in status that were alleged to exist between middle-class and working-class occupations (Lockwood, 1958; Dale, 1962; Bain, 1970; Crozier, 1965). In other literature use is made of a notion connected with status, that of style of life. Here status or style of life is not seen as entering into the determination of class, but is rather considered as a crucial effect of class position. Some authors, for example, have studied patterns of kinship, friendship, family aid and the internal relationships of the middle-class family (for example, Bott, 1957; Rosser and Harris, 1966; Bell, 1968; Pahl and Pahl, 1971). Investigations of educational opportunity implicitly or explicitly compare working-class and middle-class family practices in relation to the use of, and access to, educational resources (see, for example, Halsey *et al.*, 1980).

If status and style of life are no longer generally conceptualised as sources of class determination (with the notable exception of Giddens, 1973), they are none the less seen as partial explanations of action or consciousness (but see Bain *et al.*, 1973). Blain (1972), for example, in his study of the unionisation of airline pilots, did not expect pilots to be particularly militant given their general political attitudes. However, the radical action taken by the pilots' union is mainly to be explained by the status concerns of the pilots who felt they were not properly recognised as professionals by airline companies. A similar, more general, point is made by Lumley (1973), who argues that status concerns have been important in the aims and behaviour of middle-class unions even if they have not been significant in the growth in membership. It is to these latter points that we now turn.

The most important way in which action by the middle class is researched in the literature is in the many investigations of white-collar trade unions (although for further discussion of middle-class politics see Chapter 8). The critical issue here is whether white-collar trade unions are different from manual trade unions, reflecting the different class bases of their membership. If the characters of the two kinds of unions are more or less the same, it would give an additional dimension to the proletarianisation thesis.

The basis for discussion of white-collar trade unions lies in the increase in union membership in these occupations during the whole of the period 1948–74, while the membership of manual unions remained largely static (see Table 3.1). However, the growth in absolute numbers of members is not a particularly revealing datum. Of more significance is union density, that is, the proportion of persons employed in a given occupation who are union members. When the changes in size of the white-collar and manual labour forces are taken into account, the increase over the period is not so striking, although there is still an increase in overall union density between 1948 and 1974, more pronounced in white-collar than in manual occupations. In 1964 white-collar union density was about 30 per cent and in 1974 it had risen to about 40 per cent.

There are notable variations in white-collar union density from industry

Table 3.1: *The Growth of White-Collar Unionism in the UK*

| | Union membership (thousands) | | | | % Increase | |
	1948	1964	1970	1974	1948–74	1970–74
White-collar	1,964	2,684	3,592	4,263	+117·1	+18·7
Manual	7,398	7,534	7,587	7,491	+0·1	-1·3
	Union density (%)				% Increase	
	1948	1964	1970	1974	1948–74	1970–74
White-collar	30·2	29·6	35·2	39·4	+9·2	+4·2
Manual	50·7	52·9	56·0	57·9	+7·2	+1·9

Source: Price and Bain, 1976, p. 347.

to industry and between men and women. Densities are relatively higher in government service, both local and national (at about 80 per cent); rather lower in education and the media (between 40 and 50 per cent); and lowest in manufacturing (12 per cent) and distribution (15 per cent). Generally, the density of unionisation among men is greater than that for women (36 as opposed to 25 per cent). This difference is reflected in most branches of industry. In education and insurance, banking and finance, for example, the proportion of men unionised is double that for women. The significant exception to this sex difference is in government where densities among women are higher, especially in local government (data from Lumley, 1973, table 2.3, p. 28). Differences of this kind, and differences between manual and white-collar unionisation, have provided the basis for testing various hypotheses concerning the determinants of union membership. After an exhaustive review, Bain (1970) concluded that differences in sex composition, age, class of origin, status, earnings and promotion prospects do *not* explain differences in the propensity of manual workers to join unions (see also Bain *et al.*, 1973; Lumley, 1973). The factors that best explain unionisation are degree of bureaucratisation and extent of mechanisation. As we have seen, these two factors are, in practice, closely linked, since the reorganisation of office employment has meant the introduction of automated methods in the context of increased bureaucratisation. Clearly such a finding could be used to support a version of the proletarianisation thesis, but only on the assumption that the propensity to join a union is an index of the acquisition of 'proletarian' attitudes. Bureaucratisation and mechanisation both lead to a proletarianised work situation and to proletarianised action. (See Blackburn and Prandy, 1965, for a similar conclusion on the role of bureaucracy in fostering unionisation.) Bain also concludes that certain 'external' factors, namely, the attitudes of employers towards unions, and government policy, will affect union density.

However, it can be argued that union density is not necessarily a good guide to militancy or proletarianisation. Blackburn (1967) suggests that the character of a union should also be taken into account. Character, or unionateness, is estimated by reference to seven features of union activity. A union is more unionate (more 'radical') if it regards collective bargaining as its main function, is independent of employers in negotiation, is prepared to use industrial action, declares itself to be a trade union, is registered as a trade union, is affiliated to the Trades Union Congress, and is affiliated to the Labour Party. If one takes unionateness together with degree of unionisation (or completeness), one then has a useful measure of the significance of union membership. Despite the technical difficulties of measuring unionateness, Blackburn concludes that there is not a great deal of difference between white-collar and manual unions in their essential character. If there are differences, they are only of degree and are simply due to the fact that 'the conditions of unionism ... have not affected white-collar workers to the same extent that they have manual workers' (Blackburn and Prandy, 1965, p. 119). As soon as white-collar occupations are bureaucratised and mechanised to the same degree as manual ones, one may expect white-collar unions to be as unionate and complete as manual ones. Again, similarity of white-collar and manual unions can be used to lend support to a proletarianisation thesis. Bain *et al.* (1973), while appearing to object to the views of Blackburn on unionateness, actually add further to the picture of white-collar unions described so far. They suggest that there are no differences in unionateness, not only between white-collar and manual unions, but also between these and professional associations. In so far as there are any differences in completeness of membership, these are not attributable to class. There is no reason to suppose that social classes will behave differently if all other factors promoting unionisation, chiefly bureaucratisation, are held constant. Many members of the middle class do not have a principled objection to trade unions – they just have not considered the possibility of joining. Clearly one interpretation of this finding is that white-collar and manual unions do not represent groups whose class position is all that different. Similarity of condition entails similarity of action.

From his study of the industrial behaviour of British civil servants, Kelly (1980) reaches conclusions similar to those of the more general studies. He suggests that three groups of workers, managers, scientists and clerks, have responded very differently to changes within the civil service. Clerks have become more like a manual trade union, with a strike policy, the use of militant action and close links with the TUC. The scientists, on the other hand, have behaved more like a professional association. The activities of the managerial association have been something of a compromise between these two positions, although recently it has taken up a more militant posture. In Kelly's view, a greater unionateness does not necessarily result in an increased class-consciousness. Increased militancy has instead focused around pay issues which may in turn reflect the relative decline in civil service pay. Other factors have also been important in the development of 'instrumental unionism', in particular mechanisation and bureaucratisation. Kelly argues too, that the most militant grades are also the most feminised and, although it is difficult to disentangle this effect from others, the likelihood is that, contrary to much conventional wisdom, feminisation is one cause of a more militant trade union posture.

THE BOUNDARY PROBLEM

It is argued within the Incompatibility Thesis that Weberian analysis, in taking market chances as the fundamental determinant of class, tends to make arbitrary distinctions between occupational groups in order to produce boundaries between distinct classes. We have tried to show how this argument might apply to those authors considered in Chapter 2.

Some Weberians recognise the Boundary Problem as a genuine difficulty. Giddens, in particular, sees it as a major obstacle in the way of utilising Weber's theory of social class (see above, pp. 25–6). Parkin (1979) suggests that any solution to the proper location of the boundaries of classes will in turn raise the problem of the salience of cleavages within classes. From the point of view of the Incompatibility Thesis, Parkin's own solution, that of closure, is as arbitrary as any orthodox Weberian theory, for there is no general account possible of where closure lines come. While the more theoretically inclined Weberians, such as Giddens or Parkin, may at least discuss the Boundary Problem, it is not generally recognised as a serious difficulty. Generally, class boundaries are seen as typically fuzzy (like the manual/non-manual distinction) and it is simply impossible to decide precisely where the boundaries come.

More important, however, the characteristic Weberian response, implicitly if not explicitly, depends on a particular view of the sociological method. That is, most of the authors discussed in this chapter and the last would not see anything improper in defining classes in terms of clusters of attributes empirically found in societies. There is no sense in which classes can be specified in advance of, and independently of, empirical investigation. This 'empiricist' view of class at times becomes confused with another, and rather different, account of sociological method, which involves treating classes as nominal categories. Classes then become 'matters of definition', convenient only for the explanation of some other phenomenon. One definition of class is intrinsically as good as another and one selects that definition that is best suited to the problem in hand. To some extent the difficulties involved in the definition of class are related to the problems of relating theory to research (see Gross, 1949). That is, there may well be a gap between 'theoretical' conceptions of class and the indices of class (occupational categories, for instance) used in actual empirical research.

The Boundary Problem is also related to more fundamental considerations. Westergaard and Resler (1975), for instance, take an 'empiricist' standpoint in that they argue that class boundaries will appear only as empirically given discontinuities in the array of inequalities present in society.

We shall not tie ourselves to rigid definitions of class groupings and their boundaries, fixed in advance. To recognize the force of class division implies no commitment to an arbitrary assertion of particular lines of division from the outset. We start with the view that class 'in itself' is manifest as a set of closely related inequalities of economic condition, power and opportunity . . . We start also with an assumption that property and property relations play the key part in forming the contours of inequality. But we take that, not as a self-evident proposition, but as a highly plausible and theoretically well-grounded hypothesis, to be demonstrated by concrete evidence. (p 27)

A more usual approach is to stress the utility of the class concept in the explanation of social phenomena. Giddens, for example, criticises Weber for not providing a method for reducing the number of social classes to a point where they could be usefully used in the explanation of social processes. Lockwood argues that '"class", like any other sociological concept, is a device by which social facts are to be understood, and, in the last analysis, the definition of class that is adopted can be justified only by its usefulness in the explanation of particular and concrete events' (p 213). K. Roberts *et al.* (1977) similarly argue that the concept of class is really a matter of definition and it is a question of choosing that definition that is most illuminating.

The question 'what is social class' is really incapable of definitive answer . . . It is worth pointing out the fundamental concern of the classical writers, including Marx, in expounding their definition of social class, was to explore the inter-relationships between the economic, political, and other factors involved in systems of stratification. These are the real issues . . . Arguing about definitions is an unnecessary distraction. (pp. 17–18)

In these two chapters we have surveyed the main contributions to a Weberian analysis of the middle classes. We shall next consider the main contributions to a Marxist understanding and we shall continue to use the generic term 'middle classes' to denote a variety of different concepts employed by various writers.

4
Marxist Approaches I: Proletarianisation

As in the last chapter, it is helpful to divide the analyses into those which argue for the actual or potential proletarianisation of the middle classes and those which argue for their non-proletarianisation. This distinction in part overlaps with another, namely, between analyses which presume that there are merely intermediate strata which have no particular class character, and analyses which presume there is a distinctive class with particular interests. In both cases, though, the essential problem is taken to be that of the relationship of such strata or classes especially to the working class, and whether it will form part of a proletarian class-for-itself.

We begin this examination with a very brief discussion of Marx's own writings and then consider various proletarianisation theories, beginning with those of Corey and Klingender from the 1930s. In the next chapter we shall consider those theories which argue that the middle class has a distinctive character and that it is relatively unlikely to experience proletarianisation. Incidentally, it should be noted that there are, to some extent, different referents of the term 'middle' class. We shall try to bring out these differences which are in part related to the different national traditions and conjunctures within which the various theorists have written (see Wright, 1978, for a useful review).

MARX AND THE MIDDLE CLASS

In the *Manifesto of the Communist Party* (Marx and Engels, 1967) it is argued that in the capitalist epoch there both has been, and will be further, a polarisation between the 'two great hostile camps', the bourgeois class and the working class. The petty bourgeoisie, the small producers, artisans and craftsmen, will gradually disappear as a significant class. The lines of conflict will be clearly antagonistic, workers will be set against capitalists, and the middle class will join one or other of the hostile camps.

Now Marx and Engels have been criticised for neglecting the growing importance within developed capitalist societies of the so-called new middle class (see Dahrendorf, 1959, pp. 51–7). This is in part unfair, since on a number of occasions (apart from the *Manifesto*) Marx indicates both the general importance of classes other than capitalists and workers and the specific growth of a new petty bourgeoisie (see discussions in Harris, 1939; Nicolaus, 1967; Urry, 1973b). Thus the development of the joint stock company leads to the increasing separation of the labour of management from the ownership of capital; this labour of superintendence is conducted by an army of 'officers (managers) and NCO's (foremen, overseers), who command during the labour process in the name of capital' (Marx, 1976, p. 450). Furthermore, there is an increased importance of trade and hence of 'direct commercial agents of the productive capitalist, such as buyers, sellers, travellers' (Marx, 1959, p. 290).

Marx also says:

> The more developed the scale of production, the greater, even if not proportionately greater, the commercial operations of the industrial capital, and consequently the labour and other costs of circulation involved in realising value and surplus-value. This necessitates the employment of commercial wage-workers who make up the actual office staff. (Marx, 1959, p. 299)

Indeed, with developed capitalism and the advance of productivity, Marx envisages the time when 'only one third of the population takes a direct part in material production, instead of two thirds as before' (Marx, 1919a, p. 189). Hence, although Marx severely criticises Malthus's proposals for artificially enlarging the number of unproductive workers to consume the growing surplus, he thinks that Malthus's hope that the 'middle class will grow in size and that the working proletariat will make up a constantly decreasing proportion of the total population' is in fact 'the course of bourgeois society' (Marx, 1919c, p. 61; and see Nicolaus, 1967, pp. 42f.). Ricardo, by contrast with Malthus, was a bitter enemy of such unproductive labour – constituting so many 'faux frais de production'. But, according to Marx, what Ricardo ignores is 'the constant increase of the middle classes, who stand in the middle between the workers on one side and the capitalists and landed proprietors on the other side, who are for the most part supported directly by revenue, who rest as a burden on the laboring foundation, and who increase the social security and the power of the upper ten thousand' (Marx, 1919b, p 368).

It is therefore clear that Marx was aware that the 'middle classes' would increase in size, both absolutely and relatively. But it is also clear that he paid insufficient attention to the consequences that this development would have. In the last quote, he talks of such a development increasing the 'social security [sic] and the power of the upper ten thousand', presumably because it would act as a kind of buffer between the two major classes. But nowhere does he analyse this effect in any detail – namely, just what is the political significance of a non-labouring class constituting one-third or perhaps one-half of the population? Does it undermine or at least weaken the chances of proletarian revolution?

Many Marxists have assumed that it does not. The middle class (or classes) is/are seen as a fundamentally unstable grouping possessing neither the will nor the power to transform society (see Harris, 1939, p. 356). It is vacillating, and if the working class is well organised and the middle class effectively proletarianised, then most of the latter will come over to the side of the former. Support for this 'proletarianising' interpretation is found in Marx's adumbration of how the division of labour in the office and of the growth of public education devalues white-collar employment:

> The commercial worker in the strict sense of the term, belongs to the better-paid class of wage-workers – to those whose labour is classed as skilled and stands above average labour. Yet the wage tends to fall, even in relation to average labour, with the advance of the capitalist mode of production. This is due partly to the division of labour in the office, implying a one-sided development of the labour capacity, the cost of which does not fall entirely on the capitalist, since the labourer's skill develops by itself through the exercise of his function, and all the more rapidly as division of labour makes it more one-sided.
>
> Secondly, because the necessary training, knowledge of commercial practices, languages, etc., is more and more rapidly, easily, universally and cheaply reproduced with the progress of science and public education the more the capitalist mode of production directs teaching methods, etc., towards practical purposes. The universality of public education enables capitalists to recruit such labourers from classes that formerly had no access to such trades and were accustomed to a lower standard of living. Moreover, this increases supply, and hence competition. With few exceptions, the labour-power of these people is therefore devaluated with the progress of capitalist production. Their wage falls, while their labour capacity increases. (Marx, 1959, p. 300; and see the discussion of Carchedi, pp. 60–6 below)

We shall now consider some of the Marxist interpretations which have taken up this thesis of proletarianisation.

THE PROLETARIANISATION OF THE MIDDLE CLASS
BETWEEN THE WARS

Two of the most exhaustive accounts of the proletarianisation of the middle class, by Corey and Klingender, were, not surprisingly, produced in the 1930s (both published in 1935; see also the more polemical Brown, 1936).

Corey (1935) thought that capitalism was in its death-throes and that there was a simple choice between socialism and barbarism. The middle class, which in the past had contributed greatly to the growth and realisation of capitalist civilisation, had become mainly propertyless by the 1930s. For example, between 1930 and 1932 one out of six 'independent enterprises' was driven out of business (Corey, 1935, p. 24). Even by 1927, over two-thirds of the middle class were dependent salaried employees (p. 141). Hence the crisis was not simply a crisis of property but increasingly one of employment. The greater part of the middle class was becoming one with the dispossessed workers. The propertyless majority was sinking into lower and lower standards of living. Both the working and the middle class were engaged in a struggle for survival. The middle class in particular had been transformed into a mere aggregation of intermediate groups – and the majority (dependent salaried employees) 'must necessarily unite with the larger class of the proletariat' (p. 165). This was both because they shared the same insecurity of employment and because they performed relatively routine tasks within large economic collective organisations (p. 181). Since the new middle class was propertyless, there was, according to Corey, no reason for this class to defend property. He argues that they were simply becoming proletarian. He says:

> Lower salaried employees and professions . . . are forced to adopt pro-letarian forms of action: unions, strikes, mass demonstrations, labor party, all moving towards the communist struggle for power and socia-lism – the final logic of their proletarianisation and identification with collectivism . . . [they] are not 'allies' of the working class, they are part of the working class and its struggle for socialism. (p. 344, text and footnote)

Corey thus concentrates mainly on the overall changes in the structure of Western capitalism which were transforming the market situation of salaried employees. He does not refer in much detail to changes in the labour process for such workers, except to quote from Speier (1952, first published 1934). In this article Speier first details the tremendous growth in white-collar employment in Germany in the first quarter of the century – it increased from 6 to 10·9 per cent of all those gainfully employed bet-ween 1907 and 1925, of whom over half were women (Speier, 1952, pp. 70–1; see also Lederer, 1912). Secondly, he attempts to account for this development in terms of the following causes: the increasing importance of distribution rather than production, there being less possibility of rationalising and saving labour in distribution; the growth of 'specialised preparations for production' and hence of 'a hierarchy of technical sala-ried employees' (Speier, 1952, p. 72); the increased use of scientific man-agement and hence of planning, administrative and control functions; and the growth of organisations and associations to represent particular corporative interests. And thirdly, he assesses the consequences of these developments – in particular that the increasing size of the category decreases its social level. In particular, Speier analyses the feminisation of clerical labour, and how women tend to perform mainly subordinate roles. Indeed, the numerical growth in salaried employees is especially traceable to a demand for subordinates rather than fully qualified responsible persons. The majority of such subordinates perform duties which are 'specialised and schematised down to the minutest details'. No general training is required – only a 'very limited and brief training' (p. 73). The personal experience of the individual worker is progressively replaced by a rational scientific business administration – one consequence being that workers can be hired and fired without danger to the enterprise's efficiency. Speier talks of 'unskilled and semi-skilled salaried workers, whose designation already indicates the assimilation of the processes of work in the office to that in the factory' (pp. 73–4). He also points out, like Corey, the growing insecurity of such workers, as well as their increased recruitment from strata generally considered inferior in social esteem.

However, Speier, unlike Corey and, as we shall see, Klingender, does not consider that this class is simply becoming proletarianised. There are important sources of superior social esteem which serve to demarcate it from the working class proper, although much white-collar work can be viewed as similarly deskilled, routinised and fragmented. Such social esteem is derived from their education, as co-bearers of science and culture, from their share in the authority of those who rule in the enterprise, and from their share in official national authority. Speier thus interestingly points to some of the considerations which, as we shall see, Poulantzas employs to demarcate the 'new petty bourgeoisie' (see below, pp. 69–75).

However, Corey and Klingender both employ Speier to support a proletarianisation thesis. Klingender (1935), whom we shall now consider, forcibly argues that there are only strata intermediate between the capitalists and workers. These strata do not constitute a class because they do not perform a specific economic function. They are characterised by vacillation – yet because of their growing size they will significantly determine future political alignments.

Klingender analyses in particular the changing conditions of clerical labour in Britain (see also Anderson 1976, on this). By the end of the nineteenth century he suggests that a new, specifically capitalist character of clerical employment had emerged. The older patriarchal relations between master and men had been shattered. By 1900 the wages of clerical workers were more or less assimilated to those of skilled workers. And so by the period 1900–14, Klingender argues, proletarianisation was complete and 'the first cracks were appearing in the alliance that cemented the clerks to the ruling class' (p. 24). Four particular features are noted: first, increasing feminisation so that by 1911 one-quarter of clerical workers were female; secondly, the youthfulness of clerks – in 1911 half were under 25; thirdly, the loss of the educational monopoly of the middle classes resulting from the 1870 Education Act; and fourthly, the rationalisation of labour consequent upon centralisation and concentration within the banks and insurance companies (pp 17–22). In the immediate post-war crisis, this led to considerable trade union activity among clerical workers, to some extent following the example of the large manual trade unions. And for the 1920s Klingender discusses the twin processes of office rationalisation and mechanisation. On the first, he says: 'The amalgamation process created the monster office in which vast numbers of clerks are herded together for their daily work . . . By the resulting specialization of clerical functions it increased the productivity of clerical labour'. And, on the second, he talks of the 'technical proletarianization of clerical labour . . . it is the advent of the office machine, after the establishment of the office factory, which vitally transforms the work of the clerks and finally destroys the former craft basis of their trade' (p. 61). He discusses how the introduction of the typewriter led to the elimination of male copyists, or clerks; while the growth of various machines related to book-keeping and invoicing transformed the labour process in most offices. By 1930 the average clerical wage was approximately the same as that for skilled manual workers (p. 79), while there were dramatically increasing rates of clerical unemployment (pp. 91f.). As a result, according to Klingender, clerical workers acquired the last decisive characteristic of the wage worker, that of uncertainty with regard to the future. He concludes:

> The ultimate alliance of the middle strata with the working class is a historical necessity arising directly from the identity of their basic interests as opposed to those of the capitalist. The isolation of these strata from the capitalist class and an alliance of their most advanced section with the workers is a condition for the conquest of power by the working class. (p 103)

This literature is clearly of considerable interest. It does, however, suffer from a number of deficiencies. First, nowhere is it established just what constitutes 'proletarian' interests – this is simply assumed. Secondly, it does not follow that the middle class strata, even if proletarianised economically, will necessarily take up proletarianised political positions (see Rowse, 1931, p. 68, on the sources of political conflict between the lower-middle and working classes). What kind of coalition is it therefore possible to establish? Thirdly, the analysis of the labour process of white-collar workers is extremely brief. It is, for example, incorrect to suggest that the only tendencies are towards rationalisation and mechanisation in existing clerical labour processes.

We shall next discuss some later versions of the proletarianisation thesis beginning with the postwar debate in France and the analysis of the *couches intermédiaires* – a discussion particularly related to the second criticism above. Investigation of the third criticism will be conducted by analysis of the Braverman debate on deskilling. In the final section of this chapter we shall consider the most sophisticated version of the proletarianisation thesis which is focused upon more detailed analysis of the 'collective labourer'.

INTERMEDIATE STRATA

It is worth noting that the growth of the new middle class occurred rather later in France than in Britain, Germany, or the USA. It is to an important extent a post-Second World War phenomenon. Furthermore, this was a period in which political debate was particularly polarised between left and right and, within the left, between communists and socialists. As a result there has been a particularly lively discussion in France as to the class nature of this recently developed social grouping. Moreover, much of this debate has been located within a Marxist framework, namely, whether this new middle class will take up a proletarian class position and how this is to be achieved.

The orthodox position on the French left has been that advanced by theorists of the French Communist Party (PCF) as part of their analysis of state monopoly capitalism (see Ross, 1978, for a very helpful overview: and PCF Traité, 1971). They commence from the fundamental position that there are only two real classes within capitalism, the bourgeoisie and the proletariat. Between them are a wide variety of *couches inter-médiaires*, which do not form a class, or even a number of classes, but constitute merely a number of differentiated and fairly unconnected strata. The PCF considers that there is a long-run historical process which will mean that these strata will ultimately take up a proletarian position. The factors that will bring this about include: (*a*) the undermining of notions of independence and status because these workers are increasingly salaried rather than paid by fees; (*b*) the increased intensity and insecurity of employment as efforts are made to reduce and rationalise such technically 'unproductive' labour; and (*c*) the growing difficulty in drawing a simple division between 'workers' and 'intermediate' strata because of the development of the 'collective labourer'.

However, although these developments will mean that these strata are sympathetic to a proletarian position, this does not mean that they will automatically adopt a revolutionary form of politics. It is necessary to form an alliance and this will necessitate compromise on the part of the working class and its political representatives. It is necessary, it is argued, for the working class to moderate its demands so that it can form an alliance with the increasingly proletarianised intermediate strata. It has been this analysis which has been in part responsible for the generation of the Eurocommunist strategy, both in France and in other European communist parties (see Carrillo, 1977, for a very clear example).

There are, though, a number of problems with these claims. First, in rejecting the notion that the middle class is the third force which lies between the capitalists and workers, the PCF goes to the opposite extreme of maintaining that these intermediate strata share no interests which might unite them. It thus in effect adopts a market-based theory in which these strata are distinguished from each other by virtue of their different market capacities. Hence it ignores certain common bases of interest which are shared: in particular a degree of distance from both capital and labour. Further, the factors which will supposedly bring about the adoption of a proletarian class position do not seem adequate for the task. In certain cases they may lead to the adoption of a working-class position, but only exceptionally and for limited issues. Hence, there could be considerable costs incurred from the attempt to pursue an anti-monopoly alliance, namely (1) accusations of opportunism, (2) alienation of important working-class support, (3) failure to attract sufficient *couches intermédiaires*. And finally, it is not made clear just what constitutes the proletarian position. Little or no analysis is provided of how this may be in part transformed through the effectiveness of political action by the intermediate strata. Thus the PCF position is unsatisfactorily economistic and static. The only important source of change is seen to be rooted within the economy (see Balibar, 1977, p. 230, for a far less static and 'legalistic' conception of alliance).

A deficiency of all the approaches so far considered is that inadequate attention is paid to the more detailed changes in the labour process of specific middle-class strata. In the next section we shall therefore analyse Braverman's labour process version of the proletarianisation thesis.

Deskilling the Middle Class

We shall not summarise in detail the general thesis that Braverman advances (see Braverman, 1974, 1976; Burawoy, 1978; Cutler, 1978; Edwards, 1978; Elger, 1979; and many others). Suffice it to say that, for Braverman, it is the accumulation of capital which fundamentally determines the organisation of the capitalist labour process, and in particular the tendency for labour to become progressively fragmented and deskilled, and for the work of 'conception' (mental labour) to be separated off from the work of 'execution' (manual labour). (See Braverman, 1974, p. 20, on how the 'social form of capital . . . completely transforms technology'.) These processes occur because of the tremendous savings in the cost of labour that capital can thereby obtain. Through the so-called Babbage principle, capital can increasingly obtain precisely these quantities and qualities of labour that it requires (see Babbage, 1832, as well as Lederer, 1912, on the degree to which salaried employment is 'intellectual'). And it is within the stage of 'monopoly capitalism' that these processes have been most developed. The main features of this stage are: vast monopolistic corporations, the organisation of workers by a complex administrative apparatus, the development of a universal market, the growth of the state, the extension of an industrial reserve army, and the increasing separation of conception and execution. It is within the context of monopoly capitalism that Braverman locates the changes in the labour process of certain 'middle-class' occupations. It is essential for his thesis of a progressive degradation or deskilling of labour that he can show that even in the case of supposedly 'educated labour' the same processes are applicable.

First, then, we will consider his analysis of clerical labour (see Braverman, 1974, pp. 293–358).

He begins by noting the vast increase in clerical labour (in the USA from 0·6 per cent of the gainfully employed in 1870 to 18 per cent in 1970), and important changes in its nature. The lack of continuity with the clerk of the first half of the nineteenth century is indicated both by dramatic feminisation (75 per cent female in 1970 in the USA) and by the decline in relative pay (by 1971 median weekly earnings in the USA were less than all categories of manual labour). He suggests that in the earlier period clerical work can be likened to a craft, a total occupation, the object of which was to keep current the entire records of an enterprise and its dealings with the external world. But with the growth of the modern corporation these various functions (accounting, record-keeping, planning, correspondence, interviewing, filing, copying, etc.) were separated off into distinct departments. And at the same time there was a huge increase in purely clerical enterprises, especially those which involved the accounting of value. Braverman says that a society based on the value-form will surrender more and more of its working population to the complex ramifications of the claims to the ownership of value (p. 304).

He then considers the proposals made for the rationalisation of office work, especially with its reorganisation as a continuous flow process. This is particularly easy to effect because of two aspects of clerical labour (see p. 315). First, since such clerical operations are conducted mainly on paper, they can be easily rearranged, recombined and moved from place to place. (We could add to this the contemporary importance of computerised information in which the physical movement of material objects is rendered unnecessary.) Secondly, much of the raw material of clerical work is numerical in form and this means that mathematical controls may be used to regulate and organise the flows of work between offices.

Originally, of course, the whole office was the centre of mental labour – but with the growing rationalisation of labour the function of conception is located within an ever-smaller group in that office. The rest of clerical labour is separated off from the mental component and consists of the execution of progressively deskilled, fragmented and externally controlled manual tasks (see Glen and Feldberg, 1979, pp. 63–8). Braverman illustrates this by referring to Babbage's famous analysis of the deskilling of the mental labour involved in the preparation of mathematical tables (see Babbage, 1832, pp. 191–202; Braverman, 1974, pp. 316–19). Braverman points out how the same principles of scientific management came to be extended to office work as were already applied to shop floor work.

Perhaps the most interesting analysis is the account of the development of the labour processes within the computer industry (see Braverman, 1974, pp. 327–41; Greenbaum, 1976; Kraft, 1979). In the 1940s and early 1950s the data-processing industries displayed craft-like characteristics.

Installations were fairly small, and the tabulating craftworker operated all the machines. However, very soon a new division of labour was introduced and the destruction of 'the craft' greatly increased. A fairly rigid hierarchy developed, with startlingly different levels of pay. Entry into the higher-level jobs did not result from all-round craft training. There was a marked concentration of knowledge and control in a minute proportion of the hierarchy. Moreover, computerisation does not only affect those who work directly on the computers. All the materials produced within the office must take an appropriate form, and must be fed into increasingly automated machinery. The general level of skill required is substantially reduced – indeed, much work now requires almost no training at all. Braverman suggests that the greatest single obstacle to the proper functioning of the office is the concentration of information and decision-making capacity in the minds of key clerical employees. The recording of such information in an increasingly mechanical form will thus undermine this concentration, and will ensure the progressive deskilling of the vast majority of the clerical labour force. They are, for Braverman, unambiguously proletarianised wage workers. (See also Glenn and Feldberg, 1979, pp. 57f.; and Duncan, 1981, on the effects of microelectronics.)

In a further chapter Braverman analyses the changing labour processes of service workers, including those in the retail trade; and he argues that for all the rhetoric of a post-industrial society, most service workers are deskilled, economically proletarianised and thoroughly degraded. In the final chapter he shows, first, that a great deal of contemporary labour is overqualified; secondly, that this is obscured through the use of conventional occupational classifications (especially that of 'semi-skilled' to refer to any labour using a machine); thirdly, that the growth of education cannot therefore be simply explained in terms of economic or technological requirements, and fourthly, that high levels of education in their labour force may well be a liability for many employers. Braverman does not however explore this further except that he expects the general deskilling of educated labour to continue.

What, then, are the main deficiencies of this thesis as applied to the 'middle classes'? First of all, he does not elaborate in detail the mechanism by which deskilling is generated (see Elger, 1979). It is supposedly derived from the process of capital accumulation but this link is relatively unspecified. Indeed, all he really shows is that gains will follow for the 'employer' if certain deskilling tendencies are implemented. Yet it is not shown just how the social relations of capitalist production will *in particular* generate particular tendencies to deskilling. Nor does he even show that such changes *are* systematically introduced – much of his evidence consists of pronouncements by commentators which suggest that gains for capital would occur if these changes *were* to be made.

A further deficiency relates to his failure to consider both the forms of resistance to these tendencies to deskill, and how deskilling is in part an aspect of struggle which derives from particular class practices, not merely and directly from the accumulation of capital (see, among many, Burawoy, 1978; Elger, 1979; Friedman, 1977a; 1977b). Related to this is Braverman's economism, the fact that he fails to relate labour process changes to the developments in the state and to wider political struggles. This is a major lacuna in relationship to the 'middle classes', since many such workers are to be found within the state sector. There are two important points. First, because of the different level of struggle it is possible to establish a much higher degree of unionisation of such labour. This is likely to encourage the state as employee to wish to introduce new deskilling tendencies; while, at the same time, the workers are likely to be more able to resist such innovations. And secondly, Braverman simply presumes that the tendencies to deskill will be as marked as in the private sector – but this seems unlikely because the state is not located within the circuits of capitalist production in an analogous fashion. More generally, Braverman ignores a wide variety of determinants of class practices which lie outside the techniques of control devised by management (see Burawoy, 1978, pp. 270f.). These will in part structure a given group of workers and the kinds of class response that they develop. Now Braverman states that he is only going to consider the objective determinants of class (of class-in-itself), but this is clearly not viable. The analysis of class must involve that of class practices and struggles, and hence of classes to some degree 'for-themselves'; practices which may in part not merely prevent deskilling, but actually serve to define the essentially contestable nature of a given skill. This demands exploration of so-called political and ideological determinations. Indeed, it is plausible to argue that with respect to the middle class, to this class-in-struggle, political and ideological determinants are of greater significance than in the case of the working or capitalist classes. Furthermore, it should be noted that Braverman seems to assume both that there is a fairly unambiguous class interest among the proletariat, and that this will be unproblematically adopted by the newly proletarianised middle class. As we shall see, neither assumption can reasonably be supported.

Finally, we should note some deficiencies in his overall conception of the growing size, power and effectiveness of the working class as a result of this tendency to deskill. First of all, it is incorrect to see these changes as simply involving the replacement of craft labour by deskilled labour. As his discussion of computerisation shows, new kinds of labour and skill are regularly created and some of this, although integrated within capitalist production relations, will exhibit more of a craft form. (He also tends to romanticise early nineteenth-century labour in terms of the 'artisan ideal'; see Elger, 1979, pp. 72–8.)

Further, Braverman suggests both that there is a tendency to deskill labour and that there is an increasing size of the industrial reserve army

(1974, pp. 377–402). However, these tendencies may well conflict – to the extent to which the latter occurs, because of new microprocessor technology, for example, then there may be a reduction in, or at least no increase in, the proportion of highly deskilled labour within a particular capitalist economy (see Gershuny, 1978, pp. 118–24). Alternatively, although Braverman is well aware of certain changes in the spatial division of labour within the nation-state (for example, the growth of word-processing 'factories' in the suburbs) he does not consider its international aspects. Thus, it is increasingly the case that the different fractional operations of large multinational corporations are located within different societies. This can mean that the most deskilled operations will be located in the Third World, skilled work is carried out in the older industrial areas, and research, development and administration is organised within the metropolitan centre (the South East of England, for example; see Massey, 1981, on the restructuring of employment in the UK electrical industries). Again, one implication is that there will be a reduction in the proportion of deskilled labour within the metropolitan economies, as, in a sense, its working class is exported. Finally, much of the remaining deskilled labour will be female and this will be important in undermining the necessary homogeneity of the deskilled and proletarianised working class. Relations between male and female workers often involve intense struggles, especially over definitions of skill, training, seniority, and so on (see Hartmann, 1979).

For all these reasons, then, this relatively simplified proletarianisation thesis, based on the necessary deskilling of labour, does not provide us with an adequate understanding of the new middle classes. We will now consider Carchedi's more complex elaboration of the proletarianisation thesis, involving analysis not only of labour, but also of the changing organisation of capital.

GLOBAL CAPITAL AND THE COLLECTIVE LABOURER

One political implication of Braverman's thesis might be that the way to win the middle classes over to the proletariat would be to offer to restore their craft privileges that have been eroded by deskilling. Carchedi, however, argues against this reactionary position, on the ground that the new middle clas is to be located by reference not only to the labour but also to the capital functions which it fulfils. (1977). Hence, the processes of proletarianisation are singularly complex and require analysis of changes of the functions of both labour *and* capital in monopoly capitalist societies (see Urry, 1976, for a more exhaustive discussion).

The first point to note, then, is that Carchedi attempts merely an economic identification of the new middle class, and explicitly ignores the political and ideological levels (see Urry, 1981b, for a critique of the 'economic, political, ideological' model). Further, his analysis is conducted on the two highest levels of abstraction, of the 'pure capitalist structure' and of the 'capitalist socio-economic system', the latter being the totality of social relations and structures corresponding to a given economic structure. No analysis is provided at the level of the social formation. This economic structure is seen as one in which the production relations are determinant – this means that although they determine the determined instances (such as distribution, exchange, the superstructures, etc.), the latter react back on the former but in ways which are determined by the relations of production (see Carchedi, 1977, pp. 47–8, 143–60).

Carchedi argues that this capitalist process of production consists of both a labour process (LP) and a surplus-value-producing process (SVP). The former is that process by which useful labour creates, with given use-values, new use-values; the latter is that process by which value and surplus-value are produced. The capitalist mode of production (CMP) is a unity in which the former process is subordinated to the latter; use-values are produced only as a means for the production of exchange-values. The LP involves binding relations between the labourer and the means of production, the SVP involves those relations which bind these two elements with the non-labourer. How, then, do these various distinctions enable the theorisation of distinct social classes?

Carchedi suggests that the pure capitalist mode comprises four fundamental dichotomies:

(1) the productive/unproductive dichotomy, or that between the exploited (of surplus-value) and the exploiter;
(2) the non-owner/owner dichotomy;
(3) the labourer/non-labourer dichotomy as given by the social division of labour;
(4) the distributional dichotomy as 'determined' by (1) (2) (3), thus yielding a given class's share of social wealth, its mode of acquisition and its origin.

These four dichotomies enable us to define the two basic classes: the working class are the producers, the exploited, the labourers; those whose income is determined by the value of their labour-power, which is produced by themselves and paid back to them by the capitalist. By contrast, the capitalist class are the non-producers, the owners, the non-labourers; those whose income is derived from surplus-value, is limited by the extent of that surplus-value and is not produced by them but by their workers.

These points, then, provide the basis for Carchedi's theorisation of the class position of the new middle class (NMC). This theory rests on a three-stage characterisation of capitalist development: the formal subordination of labour to capital; the development of the collective labourer; and the development of the global functions of capital. The second and the third stages have major implications for the class position of the new middle class.

In the first stage there is merely a formal subordination of labour to capital, or of the labour process to the surplus-value-producing process. In this stage the capitalist enterprise consists of an assemblage of workers under one roof, each worker producing single commodities. While the production conditions are different from those under feudalism, the technical conditions remain unchanged.

In the next stage there is real subordination of labour to capital. There is a continuous revolution in the technical conditions of production. The labour process is transformed from a simple one, where entire commodities are made by one labourer, to one that is complex and scientifically organised. The production process is split into a large number of different tasks and functions and it is continuously revolutionised so that an ever-increasing mass of surplus-value is produced and realised. The final product is the outcome of this complex labour process: it is a social product produced in common by many workers, not all of whom perform manual work. Productive labourers perform one or more of the functions of the collective labourer. A double movement takes place in the determination of productive labour under this stage. First, there is restriction of productive labour to that which involves the production of surplus-value; secondly, this category is extended to include all agents performing a function of the collective labourer.

In the third stage in the development of the pure capitalist mode, there is a similar transformation of the surplus-value-producing process. What was under private capitalism the function of one person, the capitalist, becomes under monopoly capitalism a set of fractional operations which are aspects of the global function of capital. A complex organisational structure or bureaucracy develops which is not merely the result of the co-operative nature of the labour process requiring *co-ordination and unity*, but is also a result of the function of capital which involves *control and surveillance*. Co-ordination and unity is that function performed by the capitalist as part of the labour process, control and surveillance is the function performed so that surplus-value is produced – it involves ensuring that labour is performed in a disciplined, regular and continuous manner, that the means of production are properly used, that raw materials are not wasted, that surplus-value is produced, and so on. A further important change associated with the monopoly capitalist stage is the separation of legal and real ownership. Part of the structure which performs the function of global capital consists of agents who do not own and never have owned capital. Carchedi argues that we must here analyse the real ownership of capital. The true capitalists in this stage are the managers, those who possess real ownership of the means of production.

We can now turn to the analysis of the NMC. Carchedi argues that in the monopoly capitalist stage the global function of capital is performed by a class (the NMC), which neither legally owns capital, nor owns it in a 'real' sense. In performing the global function it acts collectively both in the sense that this class has a large membership and in that it acts jointly with the capitalist to perform that function. However, most important, it performs *both* the function of the collective labourer and that of global capital in varying balance. The last point is crucial. In private capitalism the bearers of the capitalist function perform both capital and labour functions but the former always dominates the latter. But in the monopoly capitalist stage, for the NMC, this is not so; for some the collective labourer function dominates, for others that of global capital. Thus, for Carchedi, the NMC is that class which, without legal or real ownership of the means of production, performs the global function of capital, and it performs this function in conjunction with the function of the collective labourer. How, then, does Carchedi understand the process of its proletarianisation?

Carchedi maintains that there are two processes by which the labour-power of the NMC is devalued (see especially Carchedi, 1977, pp. 174–97). First, there is that which results from the increased productivity in those sectors of the economy which produce, directly or especially indirectly, wage goods. This is termed wage goods devaluation, and Carchedi distinguishes two forms, the general and the partial. An example of the first would be where there is a decrease in the production costs of primary education in the developed capitalist societies so that there is a general devaluation of the value of working-class labour-power. The second occurs where there is a reduction in a specific wage good that contributes to the value of the labour-power of a particular sector of the working class; an example would be Marx's discussion of commercial workers whose labour-power is devalued through the state providing cheaper training (see Marx, 1959, p. 300). Hence, the value of their particular labour-power is tendentially reduced to the average. The second form in which the labour-power of the new whole class is devalued is termed devaluation through dequalification. This occurs where agents whose labour-power has a certain value must fill positions where a lower value of labour-power is required. The agent is therefore overqualified, and there will be a tendency for the value of the labour-power of such agents to reduce to the newly demanded value. An example is again provided by Marx of commercial workers – the increasing division of labour in the office lowering the technical content of the labour required to fulfil each task (p. 300). Carchedi considers this latter form of devaluation to be particularly important in explaining the growth of the NMC in monopoly capitalism. In particular, he analyses the importance of the reduction or the elimination of the global capital function from the NMC; hence a technical dequalification also produces a social dequalification (see summary in Carchedi, 1977, pp. 24–5). He gives as an example of this an industrial chemist who, besides performing quality control tests (function of collective labourer), is also responsible for the functions of supervision and management (global capital function). However, if certain technological changes occurred, then these tests could be conducted by agents with considerably lower skills (for example, a school-leaver rather than a graduate). But at the same time, this would involve the reduction in the degree to which the functions of supervision and management over other agents were conducted by such members of the NMC.

There are a number of difficulties in this interpretation of the proletarianisation thesis (also see Johnson, 1977b; Urry, 1976; as well as Carchedi, 1977, pp. 33–6, for a reply to some of these criticisms). First, because he only attempts to provide an economic identification of the NMC, it is difficult to know what consequences would follow from the addition of political and ideological determinations. Moreover, this does not simply affect the class position of the NMC directly, as Johnson seems to imply (1977b, p. 199) – rather it affects the 'proletariat' which the NMC is allegedly approaching. This is because the proletariat itself is not a fixed entity with a given essence and interests – it too is formed within political and ideological struggles. And, in particular, it is formed within the context of middle-class struggles, which substantially affect the proletariat itself and hence the supposed process of proletarianisation.

This *de facto* reductionism can be seen in a second problem here. Carchedi views the global capital function purely in terms of control and surveillance; there is thus some similarity with Dahrendorf's analysis of imperatively co-ordinated associations (see 1959; as well as Parkin, 1979, p. 23). However, on the one hand, this ignores the range of functions of global capital, namely: (1) the conversion of money into commodities and of commodities into money within the sphere of circulation; (2) the direct control and supervision of each productive enterprise; (3) the discovery, implementation and monitoring of technical developments in the means of production; and (4) the ensuring of the necessary quantity and quality of labour-power. It is incorrect to reduce the functions of capital merely to the control and surveillance of labour-power. And, on the other hand, Carchedi ignores the diverse forms in which this particular function can in fact be performed – there are at least four forms of managerial strategy or practice: (1) direct control as analysed by Braverman/Carchedi; (2) responsible autonomy as analysed by Friedman (1977a, 1977b); (3) bureaucratic control (see Edwards, 1979); and (4) paternalist control (see Urry, 1980).

It is necessary to investigate the complex combination of strategies employed and this will relate both to the technical indispensability of the labour-power being purchased, and to the effectiveness of the social struggles such labourers can wage. No adequate analysis of the proletarianisation of the NMC can proceed which does not investigate both how such a class will be subject to different patterns of control and surveillance compared with much of the working class, and how it is engaged in performing a variety of functions of capital (as indicated above).

Thirdly, Carchedi finds considerable problems in maintaining the distinction between the LP and the SVP. Partly he seems unsure of the nature of the distinction – he says, for example, that 'there must be two types of production relations or that production relations too can be regarded from two different perspectives' (Carchedi, 1977, p. 47; and see Johnson, 1977b, p. 205). The former claim seems implausible, and in reply to Urry (1976) he suggests merely that the 'capitalist production process can be regarded both as labour process and as surplus value producing process' with the latter dominating the former (Carchedi, 1977, p. 34). However, if this is the case then it become difficult to see how and why distinctive agents are produced who bear one process or another, and indeed why some agents actually bear both capital and labour functions. How can there be agents of the LP separate from the SVP unless the LP actually is a separate process? But there is no evidence that it is so distinct, and later Carchedi seems unwilling to make such a claim. At the level of capitalist relations, what is crucial is not that there is a partially autonomous LP dependent upon the processes of unity and co-ordination. Rather there are the functions of capital and labour, with the essential character of the process being given by the need to produce surplus-value. Labourers produce not for themselves but for capital (see Marx, 1976, p. 644). Hence, it makes no sense to say that capital performs both capital functions (control and surveillance) and labour functions (unity and co-ordination).

The final difficulty which we will deal with here concerns the distinction Carchedi makes between 'managers' and the NMC. He states that 'the global function of capital is performed by a structure a first part of which only performs this function and has the real ownership of capital, a second part of which performs this function without having the real ownership of capital, and a third part of which does not economically own capital and performs both the function of the collective worker and the global function of capital (in a variable balance)' (pp. 71–2). However, it is not clear what exactly is meant by real ownership and hence how we can distinguish between managers and the NMC. Carchedi suggests that real ownership refers to the power to get labour-power organised, together with raw materials, plant and machinery, and set it to work at an appropriate pace and intensity. Yet it is difficult to see how this differs from control and surveillance – it is merely the most concentrated form of this function. Indeed, he does not, it would seem, really provide any adequate distinction between these various categories. What he does is to note certain occupational groupings that are normally identified in contemporary capitalist social formations, and then, through the mere use of their names, presume that these separate off, in a theoretically fruitful manner, groupings with distinctive positions within the class structure. Yet since he does not explicate these differences adequately, these words have a symbolic rather than a theoretical function within the structure of his argument (see Johnson, 1977b, pp. 210–12).

Thus, although Carchedi's analysis is not without value, it is not clear quite how useful it is. In the end, it can be reduced to investigating the changing social division of labour of the NMC, and of the distinction between devaluation through dequalification and wage good devaluation. In Chapter 5 we shall consider those Marxist approaches to the middle classes which maintain versions of a non-proletarianisation thesis.

5

Marxist Approaches II: Non-Proletarianisation

We shall deal with five distinct non-proletarianising theses: the first is focused on the 'unproductiveness' of middle-class labour; the second on the distinctive political and ideological determination of the 'new petty bourgeoisie'; the third on the class location of professional workers; the fourth on the Thesis of the Professional-Managerial Class; and the fifth on the contradictory class locations of the new middle class. (We shall not discuss the earlier views of Bernstein, 1961, see especially p. 72; or the Austro-Marxists, see Bottomore and Goode, 1978, as well as the discussion of Renner on pp. 31–2.)

UNPRODUCTIVE WORKERS

We shall deal briefly here with the thesis most developed by Nicolaus (1967; and see Baran and Sweezy, 1968; Urry, 1973b; as well as the discussion in Przeworski, 1977). Nicolaus points out that with the development of capitalism there will be a substantial increase in the mass of profits, whether or not the rate of profit has tended to fall. As a result, capitalists can more easily accede to the demands by workers for higher wages, who will then be able to broaden the range of their consumption (Nicolaus, 1967, p. 36). Furthermore, the growth of this surplus 'creates an entirely new class' between the capitalist and working classes (p. 38). Nicolaus designates this the 'surplus class' and refers to 'the law of the tendential rise of a new middle class' (p. 40). This stems from the apparently obvious tendency for the productive class in capitalism to decline in size; Marx talks of an advance of industrial productivity leading to a situation where only one-third of the population takes a direct part in production, instead of two-thirds as before.

Nicolaus then asks what happens to these workers released from direct productive labour through the advance of productivity. He argues that they are employed unproductively – they make up the large and growing numbers of individuals who are essential to capitalist relations but who do not themselves constitute productive labour. They fulfil one or more functions in the vast system of financing, distributing, exchanging, improving and maintaining the commodities produced by the proletariat and appropriated by the capitalist class. However, these workers are also essential to consume the increasing mass of commodities the accumulation of capital will necessitate. Nicolaus says that surplus production requires surplus consumption and that the system would collapse if there were not a class which consumed more than it produced. The growth of the capitalist surplus produces a class of unproductive labourers. Clearly then, according to Nicolaus, there is little or no possibility of proletarianisation. These are unproductive workers – and they are necessary to organise and administer productive labour, and in particular to provide effective demand for the commodities which that labour produces.

This 'underconsumptionist' interpretation has not, however, been followed up in much detail elsewhere. Partly this stems from the criticisms that have consistently been made against such interpretations in general (for a convenient summary, see Gamble and Walton, 1976). Thus, it is incorrect to suggest that the surplus cannot be consumed in the form of constant capital rather than revenue (see Yaffe and Bullock, 1975). Furthermore, even if it is the case that there is a growing surplus, it does not follow that this is sufficient to explain the growth or persistence of the middle class. Indeed, Nicolaus fails to link together the two different elements of his explanation, what we may term the 'technological' and the 'underconsumptionist'. He simply presumes that all labour that is technologically necessary (if unproductive) is simultaneously surplus-consuming. But this functionalist interpretation is clearly inadequate – there are no good arguments put forward for thinking that there are functionally equilibrating mechanisms within capitalism which ensure that there is sufficient surplus labour both to reproduce capitalist relations and to consume just that amount of surplus which would otherwise be unconsumed. Przeworski maintains, in fact, that one cannot understand the growth of such labour without considering the various struggles that different groups have engaged in, in order to extend and protect the different forms of middle-class labour, especially that within the state sector (see 1977, pp. 389–401; and Chapter 8 below).

There are two further difficulties with Nicolaus's Thesis of the Surplus Class. First, it needs to be demonstrated, not merely asserted, that there has been such an increase (rather than a redistribution) in unproductive expenditure over the past hundred years. There are *prima facie* grounds for suspecting the claim. For example, in England and Wales in 1851, 1·4 million out of a working population of 9·4 million were unproductively employed as domestic servants (Lee, 1979). Secondly, much of the growth of the so-called service sector (which is often seen as corresponding to that which is unproductive) involves the movement of capital into certain sectors that were previously organised under conditions of petty commodity production. This capitalist commodification of these sectors has the effect of greatly increasing the 'middle class' – but only because the service sector involves very little directly manual, productive labour. Incidentally, much of this labour in fact provides 'producer services', services which are directly relevant (and productive of surplus-value) for capitalist production and are not merely luxury services for consumers (see Gershuny, 1978, pp. 92–113). Hence, some of the growth of the middle class follows from, and is part of, the process of capitalist development; it is not merely a means of unproductively soaking up the surplus.

We shall now consider a further attempt to characterise the 'middle class' in terms of unproductive labour, although in Poulantzas' formulation, political and ideological factors are systematically introduced into the analysis.

THE NEW PETTY BOURGEOISIE NPB

In this discussion we shall show, first, that Poulantzas does not break with the in-itself/for-itself problematic or with the economic determination of social classes, and secondly, that he formulates the distinctiveness of the NPB in a manner similar to that of certain Weberian approaches. Overall, he provides us with the beginning and the end of an explanation but not with the substance in between. He shows that, on the one hand, there are distinctive places within the economic, political and ideological structures, places which are neither bourgeois nor proletarian; and on the other hand, that there are political/ideological positions taken up which are not apparently assimilable to bourgeois or proletarian interests. However, he does not indicate the mechanisms which link these together, in particular through the processes of class formation and social struggle. Hence, it is not shown just what constitutes the distinctive quality of the NPB and therefore whether it will necessarily take up elements of a non-bourgeois *and* non-proletarian position.

Poulantzas aims to refute a number of distinct arguments: namely (1) that those in the NPB are essentially part of the bourgeoisie, as argued by Renner (1953); (2) that the NPB is part of a distinctive third force stabilising bourgeois society, especially with the growth of the tertiary sector (see Poulantzas, 1975, pp. 196–7); (3) that the middle classes are split into two, those with authority being part of the bourgeoisie, those without it being proletarian (see Dahrendorf, 1959); and (4) that there is no middle class, or even classes, but merely a number of intermediate strata (see above pp. 55–6, and Ross, 1978, on the position of the PCF). However, most of his explicit criticism is focused upon the last of these, and thus his arguments are to be understood within the context of the French Marxist debate on the political position of the new technical and white-collar workers. His argument against the PCF is that it is non-Marxist to argue that there are intermediate strata (*couches intermédiaires*) which do not comprise a class. Such a position is akin to 'bourgeois sociology' with its various dimensions of 'stratification' (see Poulantzas, 1975, pp. 198–9). Poulantzas' position is fundamentalist – that capitalist society is a class society and that, because everyone has a class membership, so all other forms of stratification are aspects, or elements, of class relations. But his position is distinctive in arguing against an economistic conception of classes. He says that classes are to be defined not just at the economic level, but also by political and ideological determinations. Through the employment of these three levels of structural determination, Poulantzas argues that there is a distinctive NPB, linked with the traditional petty bourgeoisie (TPB). This is argued against the PCF position in order to show the dangers of courting the petty bourgeoisie. The PCF will overestimate the possibilities of a successful coalition through failing to see what is distinctive about petty bourgeois interests. Furthermore, the promoting of such a coalition may allow 'opportunist' elements to control the PCF and to deflect that party away from proletarian interests. So Poulantzas' text has a distinct political importance – to show that the thesis of 'intermediate strata' and the proletarianisation thesis contain serious dangers for the left in France, and that this is because the PCF has failed to recognise the particular economic, political and ideological determinations which separate the NPB from the working class proper. (On the debates in France, see Ross, 1978; for Poulantzas, see 1973, 1975, pp. 13–35, 191–336, 1977, in particular; and for critiques, see Carchedi, 1977, pp. 194–6; Hirst, 1977; Johnson, 1977b; Wright, 1978).

Poulantzas' position can be put in terms of a number of basic points. First, classes cannot be defined outside class struggle, outside, that is, the antagonistic, contradictory social relationships which comprise the social division of labour. Second, classes are not to be viewed in terms of the individual agents of which they are composed, but in terms of objective places in this social division. Third, these objective places are designated by a threefold structural determination, of relations of production/ exploitation, of relations of political domination/subordination, and of relations of ideological domination/subordination. Political and ideo- logical criteria do not therefore operate merely to facilitate or to prevent the transformation of a class-in-itself into a class-for-itself; they serve to constitute social classes. Fourth, in specific conjunctures classes can take up positions distinct from these structurally defined class practices, although in such cases the class does not change; it maintains its essential class character, given at all three levels. Fifth, the NPB is to be seen as a class but not one that dissolves the central contradiction between capital and labour. It is to be distinguished in the following manner:

Economically (which incidentally still plays for Poulantzas the principal role), the NPB does not belong to the capitalist class because it neither owns nor possesses the means of production, and it does not belong to the working class because much of the NPB labours unproductively. For Poulantzas, productive labour is that which produces surplus- value while directly reproducing the material bases of exploitation; and so unproductive labour is that which either does not produce surplus-value or is not directly involved in material production (see Poulantzas, 1975, p. 216). Hence, the NPB can be defined negatively as unproductive labour, which is nevertheless exploited by capital.

Politically, the NPB is involved in supervising and managing productive labour. Its principal function is to ensure the continued extraction of surplus-value on behalf of capital. This is the case in general for the NPB – it is particularly true of foremen (*sic*) and supervisors who might have been thought to labour productively. According to Poulantzas, for these workers the political level dominates the economic so that they are *not* working class since they fulfil the function of supervision and management.

Ideologically, the NPB is also separated from the other classes. Another sector of the NPB consists of technicians and engineers who are again, on most accounts, productive labour. Yet Poulantzas argues that, through their role in the technological application of science, they are necessarily engaged in the political relations of managing and supervising the labour process. In particular, since they support and reproduce mental labour (as opposed to manual labour), they reproduce the ideological domination particularly characteristic of capitalist societies. This division, though, does not simply determine the class nature of technicians and engineers. The whole of the NPB is to be defined in terms of the monopolisation of knowledge and of the simultaneous inclusion of those who possess such knowledge, and exclusion (into the working class) of those who do not. Every form of work which takes the form of a knowledge from which direct workers are excluded is part of mental labour and hence separate from the working class. This mental labour is in fact embodied within a whole series of rituals, know-how and cultural elements that distinguish it from working-class labour. Poulantzas talks of the 'cultural symbolism' involved in mental labour (see 1975, p. 258), although he also points to the fact that there is considerable variation in the degree to which such workers share in this monopolisation of 'knowledge'. He lays particular emphasis upon the acquisition of educational credentials which serve to separate all the NPB from the working class. Schooling also teaches veneration for mental labour, by disqualifying those who will only undertake manual labour (see Poulantzas, 1975, pp. 259–70; Willis, 1977, on how working-class boys 'learn to labour'; and Chapter 6 below). However, mental labourers are, as a class, subordinate to capital, and educational establishments are in part responsible for effecting the distinction between the NPB and capital. Although experts may participate in the 'secret knowledge' necessary for production and hence make it seem that workers cannot control the labour process, that knowledge is in fact fragmented and dominated by the requirements of capitalist production.

Sixth, Poulantzas maintains that the new and the traditional petty bourgeoisies form a single class, even though the latter does not belong to the CMP but to simple commodity production. They form a single class because both of them adopt common political/ideological positions resulting from their similar relationship to the class struggle between the bourgeoisie and the proletariat. This common polarisation has the effect of forging a rough ideological unity between the NPB and the TPB. Hence, because the effect of the structure is to produce a similar ideology (based on reformism, individualism, fetishising the state, etc.; see Poulantzas, 1975, pp. 290–7), they are both parts of the same class.

Seventh, important transformations are nevertheless occurring within the NPB: considerable feminisation; income proletarianisation of certain subaltern sectors; mechanisation and disqualification of some mental labour; growth of a mental labour reserve army; and declining 'quality of life' through increasing commodification. Yet those sectors affected will not take up proletarian positions unless the petty bourgeoisie is specifically represented by working-class political organisations, and their distinctive interests and polarisation are recognised and incorporated. Correct politics can only materialise when the differences between the working class and the petty bourgeoisie are fully acknowledged.

A number of important criticisms of Poulantzas' position have been developed. However, there are some significant ideas trying to escape from certain encumbrances of both Althusserianism and the more orthodox in-itself/for-itself problematic (see Hall, 1980, for a helpful summary of the shifts in Poulantzas' work).

Initially, then, Poulantzas does not demonstrate that the NPB and TPB form a single class. He presents a partial and inadequate account of the resulting ideological formations which conceals obvious differences of interest (for example, the NPB in the growth of monopoly capital and the expansion of the state, and the TPB in the contraction of them both). Hence, in the following we shall ignore the relationship of the TPB to the NPB – and we shall only consider the structural determination of the NPB. There are the following problems.

First, Poulantzas' distinction between class determination and class position is unsatisfactory. The former is produced by the threefold structure of economics, politics and ideology, while the latter is somehow outside the structure and the concrete positions taken up depend upon certain further political/ideological factors. This is problematic in part because no further analysis is provided of the latter; Hirst provocatively suggests that 'class position' is merely a means of hedging any bets made on the basis of class determination (see Hirst, 1977, p. 135, and throughout for many of the points made below). Indeed, given that class position may diverge from class determination, it is doubtful whether Poulantzas can effectively criticise the economism of the PCF; it may be that current political positions do justify an anti-monopoly popular front. But this is also problematic because Poulantzas' much vaunted anti-economism turns out to be nothing of the kind. He boldly talks of structural determination by all three instances – yet concentrates entirely on determinations within the sphere of production. Indeed, it is not clear whether the 'political' dimension is really relevant at all, except to foremen and supervisors. Yet, if he does consider it so significant, this is at considerable cost, namely, that of dissolving the specificity of the political and the state and viewing them as characteristic of all human interactions (on this see Hall, 1980; and, in a different context, Worsley, 1973). In addition, the ideological is reduced to the division between mental and manual labour. This means the neglect of many other ideological determinations (of nationality, sexism, racism, for example), and the treatment of ideology merely as an aspect of the social division of labour. But one can only treat the mental/manual division as non-economic if one adopts a peculiar notion of the economic, namely, as referring only to the relations of production and the division of productive/unproductive labour. Hence, Poulantzas does not avoid economism. The use of the class determination/class position distinction is in effect all he provides in order to prevent an economistic conception of social classes and, as we have seen, he fails to provide any account of the conditions determining the latter. So we have an instance of the classic in-itself/for itself problematic, but without any elaboration of the conditions that might transform one into the other. Furthermore, Poulantzas, for all his rhetoric about the 'class struggle' and how classes only exist in struggle, gives no indication of how struggles may affect the overarching structures. The latter appear to march on regardless, uninfluenced by the concrete political programmes and strategies of the particular social forces engaged in struggle. Finally, his economism can be seen in the essentialist notions of capital and labour. He presumes that their class interests can be derived from their respective places within capitalist relations of production. He does not explore how the domain of 'class struggle' serves not merely to release class interests, but in part to constitute them. When he talks of political/ideological determinations this is what he is in effect signalling – that struggles have effects and that these effects are in part constitutive. However, because of his allegiance to Althusserianism, he has to adopt an overarching 'structural determinism'; and because of his essentially orthodox notions of class, he has implicitly to adopt an in-itself/for-itself problematic. There is, as we have suggested, an alternative position trying to emerge.

Another set of problems concerns the definition of the working class. Wright points out that the strict application of Poulantzas' criteria would result in less than one-fifth of the economically active population in the USA being considered working class – while 70 per cent would be in the NPB (see Wright, 1977, pp. 53–8; and the reply in Poulantzas, 1977, pp. 119–20). Poulantzas, surprisingly, does not dispute this figure, but points out *inter alia* the imperialist nature of contemporary capitalism. It is clear that a fair proportion of the working class in the Third World is employed by American capital. Thus, there are important changes in the spatial division of labour which involve transformations in national, regional and local class structures. However, Poulantzas fails to explore the consequences. To the extent to which there is a greatly reduced indigenous working class, then the problem of domestic class alliances is absolutely central. And it is very difficult to see how the NPB will not dominate any potential working-class movement, based as it appears to be, at least in the dominant capitalist economies, on a fairly small and declining working class (see Hymer, 1975, for a schematic account of spatial changes in contemporary capitalist economies).

The reason why Poulantzas ends up with such a small working class is because he adopts restrictive criteria for working-class membership. All the distinctions employed give rise to problems. The mental/manual division is very interestingly discussed, but two difficulties should be mentioned (see Wright, 1978, p. 53). First, it is unclear why this division should be considered to be a determinant of an actual class boundary. It is not obvious that there is a clear distinction here which divides the working class from the petty bourgeoisie. Skilled workers, for example, possess forms of knowledge that are embodied in various rituals and symbols which similarly exclude those not in possession. In some cases this possession is also based on appropriate credentials. There are, incidentally, interesting similarities here to Giddens's emphasis on education and training (see above, pp. 22–6). Given also that there is a division between mental/manual labour within the mental labour component, it would also seem that there is no strong divide between mental and manual labour, unless of course it coincides with the distinction in orthodox sociology between head-work and hand-work. Secondly, it is unclear why Poulantzas prioritises this particular aspect of the division of labour, except of course that it would appear to fit neatly into the 'ideology-box'. Yet the sexual division of labour, and especially the ideological sex-typing of occupations, could plausibly be argued to be of equal salience; does this make all males non-working class? (See Hakim, 1979, for some very clear evidence on this).

Finally, we should consider productive and unproductive labour, since Poulantzas' idiosyncratic formulation of the distinction is the main reason why the working class is, on his definition, so small (on this see Wright, 1978, pp. 46–50; Parkin, 1979). The first difficulty is that he confines productive labour to that which is engaged in material production. Yet this is an arbitrary definition since there is nothing about whether a use-value is physically tangible which determines whether it is produced productively or unproductively. As Marx says, 'a schoolmaster is a productive worker when, in addition to belabouring the heads of his pupils, he works himself into the ground to enrich the owner of the school. That the latter has laid out his capital in a teaching factory, instead of a sausage factory, makes no difference to the relation' (Marx,

1976, p. 644; and see Poulantzas' very weak defence, 1977, pp. 119–20). Secondly, whatever common interests might exist between 'unproductive workers', it is also necessary to consider important divisions: between the dominant and subordinate categories, especially resulting from the credentials possessed; between male and female workers; and between those working in capitalist enterprises and those working within the state. The last of these distinctions is elaborated by Baudelot, Establet and Malemort (1974). They point out that in 1968 in France the latter category was larger than the former (1,194,000 compared with 1,180,000; see p. 256). Such workers clearly have specific interests in sustaining the state, and in providing support for the notion that the state can act neutrally. The organisation of such groups within the state bureaucracies has tended to generate a greater degree of collective political orientation than among such groups within capitalist enterprises. The latter tend to be more individualistic, respectable and moderate; and more willing to oppose working-class trade unions. Increasingly, then, the 'unproductive' new petty bourgeoisie will be found outside private capital and within the state. No account of the middle class will be adequate which does not take this fully into account.

PROFESSIONS AND GLOBAL CAPITAL

In this section we shall discuss Johnson's analysis of professional workers, before considering in the next section the concept of the Professional-Managerial Class. Johnson (see especially 1977a, although his earlier book, 1972, is also of interest) in part bases his analysis upon that of Carchedi, using his categories of collective labourer and global capital to identify the specific class location of the professions. In particular he argues against Oppenheimer and Friedson (both 1973), maintaining that their different analyses are in fact both premissed upon a similar Weberian approach to social class and social development. In the case of Oppenheimer, the professions are seen to be experiencing a process of proletarianisation which results from their increasing subordination to bureaucratic authority, this process being viewed as inherent in the rationalising tendencies of large-scale enterprise. As a result the professional gradually adopts collectivist class attitudes. For Friedson, by contrast, the authority structures of post-industrial society will be dominated by professionals, by institutionalised expertise rather than by management. Professionals are thus resistant to the rationalising consequences of large-scale bureaucratic authority.

Johnson, however, argues that both writers fail to acknowledge, first, that there is a central dualism involved when knowledge is organised as work; and secondly, that this dualism is an instance of the central dualism characteristic of capitalism in general. It is only, he says, a Marxist analysis which is able to discover this underlying dualism rooted within the relations of production – the Weberianism of Oppenheimer and Friedson leads them both to equate the relations of production with the more general social division of labour and authority resulting from the conditions which effect imperative co-ordination. So Johnson tries to support two claims: first, that there is a dualism characteristic of the occupational organisation of knowledge; and secondly, that this is specifically linked to capitalist relations of production. We shall see that although the first claim is in part substantiated, the second is not.

On the first, Johnson turns to the analysis of the indetermination/technicality ratio (I/T) initially elaborated by Jamous and Peloille (1970). They say:

> The I/T ratio expresses the possibility of transmitting by way of apprenticeship, the mastery of intellectual or material instruments used to achieve a given result. This makes it possible to appreciate the limits of this transmissibility; i.e. the part played in the production process by 'means' that can be mastered and communicated in the form of rules (T), in proportion to the 'means' that escape rules and, at a given historical moment are attributed to virtualities of producers (I). c1970, p. 112)

What is distinctive to this is the emphasis placed on indetermination, or what Johnson had called the 'structure of uncertainty' (1972). Most so-called professions have a high I/T ratio. Jamous and Peloille argue that technicality, the codification of increasingly technical knowledge, does not guarantee an occupation's professional status. This is because the greater the degree to which there is a rationalised and transferable body of knowledge, the greater are the possibilities of its organisation and take-over by others from outside that occupation. This may occur, on the one hand, through another occupation attempting to undermine the already established professional monopoly – Jamous and Peloille analyse in detail how clinical doctors in France tried to prevent the loss of their monopoly on the production of medical knowledge. Or, on the other hand, if knowledge is systematised and transferable, then it can be more effectively fragmented and routinised through its location within a new, deskilled process of production.

Indetermination, by contrast, refers to the unformulateable aspects of professional knowledge; the qualities which are necessary but which cannot be expressed in codified form. Examples would include the doctor's 'bedside manner', the teacher's mystique, the basis of the lawyer's legal opinion, and so on. In each case the claim to legitimacy is based on more than a given body of codified knowledge. There are virtualities of certain occupations which are used to prevent or limit external intervention. In the case of the clinicians, Jamous and Peloille argue that they alone possessed certain 'individual and social potentialities, experience, talent, intuition' (p. 139) which were essential for the evaluation of clinical tests. Such indetermination is the basis upon which professional ideologies and legitimations are reproduced. Hence, we cannot talk of some general process or tendency to 'professionalisation'. Rather there are competing ideologies based on varying degrees of indetermination. For example, 'clinical medicine has been able to set off a professional ideology giving rise to particularism, "quality", valorization and charisma' (p. 147).

Now although this distinction seems clear, Johnson confuses the issue by defining indetermination as 'those aspects of the professional organisation of knowledge which function as barriers to intervention' (1977, p. 99). However, while this may be the effect, it is not legitimate to define indetermination in terms of this functional consequence. It must be defined in a manner which is separate from its effects. So Johnson, having somewhat misdefined indetermination, then argues that Jamous and Peloille fail to theorise its preconditions. He tries to link the I/T ratio with the overall organisation of capital and labour and specifically with Carchedi's distinctions between global capital and the collective labourer (on this see pp. 60−6 above; see also Johnson, 1977b, for a later critique of Carchedi). He maintains that at the level of the occupational organisation of knowledge, the labour process (LP) involves technicality, and the surplus-value-producing process (SVP) involves indetermination. Thus whether or not an occupation can resist bureaucratisation, routinisation and fragmentation depends on whether its work tasks are an aspect of the function of the collective labourer or the function of global capital. Where the latter is the case, where there is work of control and surveillance and especially that of the reproduction of labour-power, then the occupation is protected from those processes of work devaluation which affect the collective labourer. So, if we return to Friedson, occupational authority is only resistant to bureaucratisation and deskilling where those occupational tasks are at least in part embedded within the global function of capital. It is thus essential to theorise the conditions for indetermination/technicality at the level of production relations.

Johnson then relates this argument to two professions, doctors and accountants. (See also Johnson, 1977b, pp. 216−22, 227−32, for what amounts to a critique of Johnson, 1977a, on these points.) The first of these, the medical profession, has been able to sustain a high I/T ratio because it is centrally involved in the reproduction of necessary labour-power. In particular, it has monopolised official definitions of who is, and who is not, a fit vendor of labour-power. Thus in this case professionalism (and a corresponding large income mainly paid out of revenue) is sustained because ideological and political processes coincide with the requirements of capital. However, one difficulty with this explanation is that the function of 'control and surveillance' has had to be considerably broadened in order to incorporate the certification and reproduction of labour-power. Indeed, Johnson is his later paper notes that a set of control mechanisms is involved here which is not directly relevant to the appropriation or realisation of surplus-value (1977b, p. 228). In the case of accountancy, Johnson tries to show that there is a tendential fragmentation of the occupation, between, on the one hand, glorified book-keepers performing 'technical' functions associated with the implementation of systems of financial or stock control as part of the collective labourer functions, and on the other hand, the devisers of systems of financial control, whose knowledge is in part 'indeterminate', and who function as an element of global capital. Again, there is the difficulty that the function of capital has had to be extended to include the process of realisation of value which is not obviously implied within the conception of 'control and surveillance', except obliquely. Furthermore, it is unclear that there is anything 'indeterminate' about the knowledge required – the main barrier to external intervention lies in its esoteric technical nature and the power that flows from this. Another difficulty in Johnson's formulation lies in his suggestion that these glorified book-keepers are performing merely technical tasks associated with the collective labourer function. The problem with this is that it is not a purely technical function at all – it is a function concerned precisely with the regulation and realisation of value, and surplus-value, in other words, resulting from the SVP and global capital. Thus the accountancy 'profession' can only be understood as an occupation fragmented within capital. Therefore, as Johnson argues later, part of the new middle class consists of occupants of 'positions within the social division of labour (as structured within the process of realization) which operationalize a function of capital but do so as part of an increasingly fragmented and routinized labour process' (Johnson, 1977b, p. 218).

Although Johnson's discussion of the medical and accountancy professions is problematic, he does draw attention to the following important points:

(1) Much of the new middle class consists of workers within the state sector who are concerned with the reproduction and regulation of labour-power. The development of, and changes in, this sector cannot be reduced to the functions of capital (such as control and surveillance).

(2) A further important sector consists of those workers who provide 'producer services' (see Greenfield, 1966; Gershuny, 1978); functions necessary for capital either to produce or especially to realise surplus-value (for example, accountancy, marketing, advertising, computer services, and so on). These are generally capitalistically organised although the labourers employed are, as we shall see, 'new middle class' rather than working class.

(3) Although it is not possible unequivocally to link I/T with capital/labour functions, it is important both to distinguish between different

forms of knowledge, of different kinds of so-called 'mental labour', and to connect these with different aspects of the production and realisation of surplus-value.

(4) Professions cannot be understood only in terms of the I/T ratio, partly because this reproduces the deficiencies of the 'trait' approach (a profession consists of the following traits, *a, b, c*). Nevertheless the form of knowledge that an occupation is based upon is crucially related to its success in establishing or sustaining professional status. Certainly one factor which determines this is the I/T ratio.

(5) However, there are also high-technicality occupations – but technicality is not to be viewed as a function of the collective labourer. This is because arguing promotes the notion that technology is somehow neutral. Technology is not neutral – and hence its promotion is part of the function of capital, not of the collective labourer.

Overall, then, Johnson's attempt to theorise the class position of professionals does not succeed, although his argument does raise a number of critically significant issues. We shall now consider an alternative theorisation of professionals – one based not on their differing forms of knowledge but on the notion that they themselves form a distinctive class with managers, the Professional-Managerial Class.

THE PROFESSIONAL-MANAGERIAL CLASS

The Ehrenreichs argue that by the early 1960s it was impossible for Marxists to ignore the distinctive growth of a stratum of educated wage-labour which could not be viewed as simply proletarian (see Ehrenreich and Ehrenreich, 1979a, p. 7; generally, on this thesis, see the collection in Walker, 1979). They criticise the proletarianisation thesis (in particular, in Freedman, 1975; Gorz, 1967, 1976; Mallet, 1975), arguing that 'technical workers, "culture" producers, etc. – must be understood as a distinct class in monopoly capitalist society' (Ehrenreich and Ehrenreich, 1979a, p. 9; for empirical support with regard to managers in the UK, see Bamber *et al.*, 1975). It cannot be considered as part of the working class because it has objectively antagonistic interests. Also it is not a *new* middle class since its class position is quite distinct from both sales and clerical workers, and from the older petty bourgeoisie. This class of professionals and managers (the PMC) then, consists of 'salaried mental workers who do not own the means of production and whose major function in the social division of labour may be described broadly as the reproduction of capitalist culture and capitalist class relations' (Ehrenreich and Ehrenreich, 1979a, p. 12). The PMC thus consists of people with a wide range of occupation, skill, income, power and prestige, who nevertheless share a common function in the overall division of labour and a common relation to the economic foundations of society. The Ehrenreichs suggest that something like 20–25 per cent of the American population constitute the PMC – about 50 million people. Its existence depends upon two factors: first, that there is a sufficient surplus to sustain this non-productive class (see pp. 67–9 above for further discussion), and secondly, that a class specialising in the reproduction of capitalist class relations becomes a necessity for the capitalist class.

They argue that the growth of the PMC in the USA began at the end of the nineteenth century because certain key developments, the reorganisation of the productive process, the growth of mass institutions of social control, and the commodification of working-class life, all required professional-managerial agents for their implementation. It is these functions of the PMC which have meant that their interests contradict those of the working class – they are mutually contradictory. Furthermore, this development was not wholly unself-conscious. The members of the PMC, in the first period of growth between 1890 and 1920, saw that capitalism needed to be reformed, and that they could function to mediate the basic class conflict of capitalist societies. However, not only were their interests contrary to those of the working class; they also developed quite intense anti-capitalist positions over, for example, academic freedom, Progressive reforms, consumer issues, the role of the expert, and so on (see pp. 21–5). Particularly important in this has been the development of the 'profession'. But neither the growth of specialised professions nor the division between 'management' and the liberal professions prevents us by about 1950 from characterising the PMC as 'a single, coherent class' (p. 28).

The Ehrenreichs then turn to the more recent period and try to connect the growth of the New Left with the development of the PMC. The latter obviously grew greatly in numbers and in financial rewards. Particularly important was the expansion and bureaucratisation of the university – which were indices not of the proletarianisation of the PMC but of its expansion and growth. And this fed directly into student radicalism which at least initially involved the assertion of the autonomy of the PMC against its incorporation into, and domination by, the capitalist class (see pp. 31–3; and Bouchier, 1978, pp. 43–80). Later, at the end of the 1960s, the radicalism was turned against the PMC and especially against the university, its centrally significant reproductive apparatus. This was in part the result of the Vietnam War but also of the growing working-class intake into the universities and the growth of the Black liberation movement. The student movement, which had been an irreducible expression of the PMC, thus turned and denounced both that class and the university which it sustained. In the 1970s two particular tendencies can be identified in the New Left: first, the 'radicals in the professions' approach which involves, while working in the liberal professions, the advancing of radical causes and the questioning of traditional PMC notions of skill, authority, hierarchy, knowledge, and so on; and secondly, the 'new communist' movement which advocates the return to the fundamentalist view of the working class and the need to build the vanguard party, and the rejection of the concerns of the New Left as 'petty bourgeois' (see Ehrenreich and Ehrenreich, 1979a, pp. 38–41).

In conclusion, then, the thesis of the PMC involves a number of claims:

(1)   Although the PMC is centrally involved in the reproduction of capitalist relations, since it consists of wage-earners, it has interests which are antagonistic to the capitalist class.

(2)   Much of the radicalism of the past two decades, especially in the USA, is the result of this opposition of interest between the PMC and the capitalist class.

(3)   There is an opposition of interest between the PMC and the working class, since the very function of the PMC within the capitalist division of labour results from its appropriation of mental labour from the working class, and its role in reproducing capitalist relations. (See also Gouldner, 1979, for analysis of the 'culture of critical discourse' generated among intellectuals and the intelligentsia – the 'new class'.)

(4)   The technocratic and/or cultural domination by the PMC has the following effects on the working class: (*a*) to deprive it of the effective means of resistance, (*b*) to lead it to see the PMC as the 'main enemy' since that is the class which generally deals directly with the working class, (*c*) to encourage anti-intellectualism, anti-liberalism, sexism and racism, since the opposite of these are thought to be embodied, to some degree at least, within the PMC.

(5)   Hence, there is no pure working class waiting to get its interests realised, and no simple and straightforward relationship that can be established between it and the PMC. The growth of the PMC has irreversibly transformed class relations.

Overall, we consider that the PMC thesis is highly illuminating and we shall take up many of these points in Part Two below. For the present we note some difficulties in the analysis. First, the Ehrenreichs do not consider and analyse the tendencies within the PMC which might entail 'proletarianisation' of their condition. Thus, in the USA, after the peak in 1971, there was a fall in demand for professional/managerial workers. There was oversupply, or what Carchedi termed 'devaluation through dequalification'. Unemployment of professionally qualified workers rose, the real income advantage of college education declined, and many graduates 'skidded' into non-managerial jobs (in 1972 almost one-third of men, and one-quarter of women; see Larson, 1980, pp. 151f., as well as Freeman, 1976). Larson suggests more generally that the PMC in the USA has recently experienced an increasingly rigidified division of labour, an intensification of labour especially with public expenditure cuts, and a routinisation by experts of many high-level tasks (that is, those with high technicality). Thus there are proletarianising tendencies at work even if they are not turning the PMC into a proletariat (it is important to emphasise the last point, to counter the proletarianisation position of Szymanski, 1979).

Secondly, it is not satisfactorily shown that the PMC constitutes a class. In effect, two criteria are employed: (1) a common function of reproducing capitalist relations; (2) a common educational (hence social and cultural) experience. But the Ehrenreichs do not demonstrate that there is a systematic overlap between these two, and hence do not show that there are not simply a large number of non-propertied labourers, bearing different educational credentials, and performing quite diverse tasks in the social division of labour. Some aspects of this will be discussed in the next section when we consider Wright's argument that there are different fragments of the PMC which do not have a common unifying interest. Thus, although the Ehrenreichs try to maintain two criteria for the designation of class, in effect they adopt a market conception, based on educational credentials. For them the PMC embraces all those possessing such credentials (in the USA a college degree), and they ignore reproduction as a pertinent criterion (see Albert and Hahnel, 1979, pp. 258–9; and pp. 22–6 above on Giddens's similar thesis). This is incidentally demonstrated by their treatment of college-educated women, who are treated as members of the PMC (to make up the 50 million) whether or not they are in paid employment.

Thirdly, they fail to show that the PMC is a class similar to that of capitalists and workers. They enthusiastically quote Thompson on how class is not a thing but a relation, but fail to explore the precise significance of this (see Thompson, 1968, pp. 9–11; Ehrenreich and Ehrenreich, 1979a, p. 10; Noble, 1979, p. 127). Thompson is at pains to argue that we cannot conceptualise capital and labour as two distinct classes, each with an independent being, and then see them as being brought into an external relationship with each other. Class is irreducibly a relation of opposites. Any one class for Thompson is defined in terms of its relation with the 'other' class. However, the Ehrenreichs cannot show that the PMC has any such relation. Hence, although we might wish to designate it a class, its importance and likely political effectiveness will be very different from that of capitalists and workers. One way of putting this is to consider the difference between 'class struggle', which is directly between capitalists and workers, and 'classes-in-struggle' (see Laclau, 1979, pp. 104–5; Urry, 1981b, pp. 66–8). A class-in-struggle consists of those occupying a common position in relation to the means of production, but it is a relationship which does not entail direct antagonism with one other social class. The PMC is thus a 'class-in-struggle'.

Finally, the Ehrenreichs do not show that the thesis of the PMC is generally applicable to all monopoly capitalist societies. They fail to analyse the spatial variation in the PMC; in particular it is proportionately larger and politically stronger in the USA than in Western Europe (see Hymer, 1975, on how this results from the dominance of American-owned multinationals). This means that the political effects will vary, and the Ehrenreichs' interestingly provocative conclusions may only be applicable to the USA. This again brings out how different theories take root within different national cultures. With the exception of Braverman, American writers have tended to emphasise the distinctiveness of these class locations between capital and labour. This can be seen further in Wright's analysis of contradictory class locations.

CONTRADICTORY CLASS LOCATIONS

Wright argues that it is unnecessary to assume that all positions within the social division of labour must fall firmly into one class or another. Instead, certain positions are to be viewed as objectively torn between classes; they are not class positions but 'contradictory class locations' (see Wright, 1978, pp. 61–96). Wright says that, just because there are a large number of positions between the capitalist and working classes, this does not mean that these form a class, as the Ehrenreichs maintain. His argument proceeds as follows. (1) There are three central processes which underlie the basic capital-labour relationship: control over the physical means of production, control over labour power and control over investments and resource allocations. (2) At the level of the CMP there are only the class positions of capitalists and workers; the former are in control in all these processes, the latter are controlled within each. (3) With the development of advanced capitalism these dimensions need no longer coincide and various contradictory class locations are generated, both between the proletariat and the bourgeoisie, and between the petty bourgeoisie and the bourgeoisie/proletariat. (4) In the former there are managers/technocrats/line supervisors, in the latter there are small employers located between the petty bourgeoisie and the bourgeoisie, and semi-autonomous employees such as researchers, professors, craftworkers, and so on, located between the petty bourgeoisie and the proletariat. (5) There are also contradictory class locations within the political/ideological apparatuses – these involve the execution of state policies and the dissemination of ideology. (6) Hence almost one-half of the employed population in the USA are in contradictory class locations, and between one-quarter and one-third occupy such locations near the boundary of the working class. (7) About two-thirds of the population constitute a basis for a socialist movement in the USA, although there are substantial conflicts of interest between the proletariat and those in various kinds of contradictory class location. (8) Thus there is no unified PMC. There are managers intermediate between bourgeoisie and capitalist, semi-autonomous employees intermediate between proletariat and the petty bourgeoisie, and superstructural workers intermediate between the formulators of state policies and ideology and those controlled by them.

There is thus no PMC with a common contradictory class location. (See Wright and Perrone, 1977, for a related attempt to explain income differences in class rather than occupational terms.)

Both Poulantzas and the Ehrenreichs have replied briefly to Wright's argument. Poulantzas (1977, pp. 118–20) suggests that if we were to take Wright seriously then capitalists could also be said to enjoy a contradictory class position – the capitalists being both workers, in that they perform necessary co-ordination and direction, and capitalists. But, as Poulantzas says, this would be an absurdity. However, this is a weak argument, since we saw that Poulantzas only avoids designating certain positions as contradictory by arbitrarily deciding that one particular aspect is primary (see above, p. 73). Hence, for those positions which are non-capitalist and non-worker, there may well be 'contradictory' aspects, although in certain cases Wright should have considered whether, in fact, one such aspect is dominant. It is no more satisfactory for Wright to maintain that there is simply a contradiction between two aspects, than it is for Poulantzas to decide arbitrarily that one aspect is primary.

The Ehrenreichs (1979b, pp. 331–2) point out that, for Wright, the working class occupies a 'determinate class location', which means that it has a 'fundamental interest' in socialism. Yet this is far too simple. What kind of socialism is implied, how is it to be achieved, what connection does this have with other interests? Indeed, to posit an interest in socialism as fundamental reduces the task of socialists to one of simply introducing this from outside. This is, as the Ehrenreichs say, more than a little problematic in the USA. Indeed, we can go further and ask whether the fundamental interests of capitalists can also be easily determined, given important differences between different fractions.

We shall now mention some specific difficulties in Wright's position. First, he concentrates upon the forms and amounts of control that an individual agent possesses. This means that, in effect, his approach is gradational, and it becomes a matter of ranking that agent with respect to the three dimensions: control over the physical means of production, over labour-power and over investments. Because the only categories of analysis which we can employ are those which are isomorphic with individual agents, we are prevented from analysing agents as bearers of specific functions, for example, of capital and labour and of their transformations. Furthermore, Crompton and Gubbay point out that it is difficult to maintain a clear division between the two aspects of possession, of control over the physical means of production and control over labour-power (1977, p. 183). In practice, they will go together. Indeed, it is not clear that control over the physical means of production is particularly significant. It seems incorrect to argue that craftworkers, because they have a degree of control over their immediate instruments of production, are any less workers. Likewise, it seems strange to claim that semi-autonomous workers are marginal between the proletariat and the petty bourgeoisie because they possess at least minimal control over the physical means of production. Why does this fact make them in part subject to petty bourgeois determination? Wright gets into difficulties of this sort because of his presumption that all individuals can be unequivocally defined, either as possessing a class membership, or as possessing a contradictory class location, as defined by the economy. Hence, he defines class purely in terms of the degree of control an individual possesses with regard to certain economic determinations. However, in certain cases, the fact that an individual only has control with respect to one process (out of three) does not make that individual any less a capitalist. Crompton and Gubbay point out that rentier capitalists, living entirely from investment income and taking no part in management, do not stop being capitalists because they fail to control the labour-power of others (1977, p. 183).

CONCLUSION

In Chapters 4 and 5 we have surveyed the most distinctive theories of the middle class within the Marxist perspective. We have devoted particular attention to Carchedi's sophisticated analysis of proletarianisation, and to Poulantzas' analysis of the structural determination of the 'new petty bourgeoisie'. In both cases their work has given rise to further investigations, especially those by Johnson and Wright. Carchedi's argument is noteworthy for the manner in which he elaborates the functions of 'capital' and 'labour', while Poulantzas brings out the importance of the role that politics and ideology play in the formation of social class. In both cases, however, there are critical gaps in their formulations and in Part Two we hope to overcome at least some of these, beginning with a re-evaluation of the Thesis of Incompatibility.

Part Two

Towards a Theory of the
Middle Class

6

Unproductive Labour, Knowledge and Credentials

INTRODUCTION

We started this book with a consideration of Marxist and Weberian theories. What we have said so far indicates, at least to the extent that it is simply put, that this is a problematic distinction. In particular, it may indicate differences in analytical style or emphasis rather than a conflict of principle. Indeed, in many respects, it is more useful to stress the similarities between the theories of class of Marx and Weber themselves (see, for example, Giddens, 1973; Hill, 1981; Turner, 1981). For example, in his use of the notion of expropriation Weber refers to a conception of class relations very similar to that found in Marx's work. For Weber (1964; and see Runciman, 1978) the separation of the worker from the means of production is at its most pronounced in the contemporary system of private enterprise. The separation is reinforced by the existence of a private bureaucracy within the firm, the concentration of workers in one space, mechanisation of work and, above all, a common work discipline. The key to discipline is free labour; 'free labour and the complete appropriation of the means of production create the most favourable conditions for discipline' (1964, p. 248). Since employers have no commitment to the worker, as the slaveowner has to the slave who represents capital, they are free to dismiss or engage workers as they choose, selecting those workers who perform best. To the discipline thus created by the free market in labour, Weber adds the point that, under the pressure of competition, profitability depends on eliminating as much human labour as possible and replacing highly skilled labour by machines. The relations of control in capitalist enterprise, generated by the separation of workers from the means of production and the institution of a free market in labour, are therefore critical to Weber's image of capitalist society and to his theory of class. As Giddens (1973) points out, power is central to Weber's view of class as based on market capacities.

If one cannot characterise Weber's theory as solely dependent on the notion of marketable skills, it is also limiting to interpret Marx as providing a theory in which the market for labour is simply structured by the relations of production. We shall argue later that any theory, including any Marxist theory, must include an analysis of the varying terms on which labour-power is sold, not the least because, as Marx showed in *Capital*, those terms are partly an outcome of the degree and forms of struggle between labour and capital. In recent Marxist literature there is an increasing emphasis on the labour market as a relatively independent factor determined by a multiplicity of forces (see Edwards, 1979; Gordon *et al.*, 1975).

Much of the discussion in the previous four chapters further illustrates the difficulties in contrasting the styles of analysis derived from Marx and Weber. First, we find great diversities within each set of writers. There are, for example, as many differences between Mills and Roberts *et al*, as Weberians, as there are between these two and a Marxist like Poulantzas. These may be quite large differences, too. Weberian writers are unable to agree on the size of the middle class, while in the Marxist literature there is considerable disagreement about how seriously, or in what ways, to take the theory of surplus-value. As a corollary of these internal differences, there are similarities between Marxist and Weberian accounts. Poulantzas and Giddens, for example, end up emphasising the size and importance of the middle class, while Dahrendorf and Braverman stress its small and relatively unimportant nature. Moreover, the manner in which Carchedi conceives of the new middle class as performing functions for capital is reminiscent of Renner's view that the service class performs services delegated by capital. However, writers whose position is more straightforwardly Weberian, Mills (1951) and Bendix (1956), for example, also advance views similar to these in seeing the authority of managers as deriving from the rights of capital.

Furthermore, many analyses in the sociology of class clearly indicate the possibility of reconciliation, implicit or explicit, between Marxist and Weberian approaches. Goldthorpe (1972), for example, points to the tendency on the part of many Marxists simultaneously to criticise 'bourgeois' social science and yet utilise its evidence. The more empirical Marxist studies become, the more they attain a 'rapprochement with social enquiry conducted in a more strictly academic style and context' (Goldthorpe, 1972, p. 343). Marxists, however orthodox their persuasions, are often forced to use 'Weberian' evidence (for a discussion see Turner, 1977).

A number of Weberian theories have theoretical consequences similar to those generated by Marxism. For example, in much the same way as Dahrendorf proposes authority as the fundamental and general feature of the class structure, Parkin (1979) proposes the concept of closure as unifying the analysis of all forms of inequality: 'By social closure, Weber means the process by which social collectivities seek to maximise rewards by restricting access to resources and opportunities to a limited circle of eligibles' (p. 44). Virtually any social attribute can be used as a basis for exclusion, the net effect of which is invariably to create one group that monopolises the rewards and another without them. As Parkin says, this puts the notion of exploitation at the heart of the analysis. In modern society the two main ways in which the dominant class maintains itself by exclusion are the ownership of property and the possession of credentials or educational qualifications. Property is not therefore the primary notion; it is only one of the ways in which exclusion can be achieved. In rejecting Marxism, Parkin does not think that property has lost its significance. On the contrary, in opposition to the view of many contemporary writers he argues that property continues to play a vital but not fundamental part. In sum, 'the dominant class under modern capitalism can be thought of as comprising those who possess or control productive capital and those who possess a legal monopoly of professional services. These groups represent the core body of the dominant or exploiting class by virtue of their exclusionary powers which necessarily have the effect of creating a reciprocal class of social inferiors and subordinates' (p. 58). Parkin's scheme therefore generates two social classes in the same way as Dahrendorf's and has to confront problems similar to those faced by vulgar Marxism. Two of these are of particular relevance, namely, the existence of a middle class, and social differentiations which are not based on property or credentials. For the first, Parkin's response is effectively to split white-collar workers into two groups, those with, and those without, credentials; we shall return to this solution later. As for the second, Parkin argues that there are forms of closure operating within the subordinate class based on, for example, race or sex, exclusions which are, however, not as important as the master closures of property and credentials. It is not clear that the methods or effects of Parkin's model are greatly different from some of those Marxists he so strongly criticises.

In sum, it has become increasingly difficult to decide what theory belongs in which camp and what general rules could establish a privileged discourse (for a recent example see Cutler *et al.*, 1977). Analysis of the middle class raises this problem particularly acutely. As 'Weberians' have become worried about the Boundary Problem, and 'Marxists' have recognised the importance of middle classes, the theoretical waters were bound to become muddy. In these circumstances it is more profitable to worry less about the way in which one discourse is privileged over another and more about the manner in which an adequate theory of the middle class can be constructed. Thus, we start, in this chapter, with an examination of how social classes are structured by the changing forms in which knowledge is organised within societies dominated by capitalist social relations. In particular, we shall try to show the interrelationships between three issues normally kept separate. These are: the changing relations between mental and manual labour, the analysis of social classes and the nature of 'organic intellectuals'. In Chapter 7 we show how this structuring of knowledge is related to the specific constitution of the work and market situations of social classes apparently 'in the middle'; and in

Chapter 8, we turn to an analysis of the role of struggle in the determination of the causes and consequences of social classes.

KNOWLEDGE AND COMMODITY EXCHANGE

Normally, where analysis is undertaken of the connections between class and knowledge, attention is directed to the way in which different social classes generate different knowledge-*contents* (as in the conventional sociology of knowledge; see Abercrombie, 1980). However, this poses the issue too simply. In particular, it is necessary to consider, not merely the different contents of knowledge, but that there are different forms in which knowledge is produced and organised; that distinct modes of economic and social organisation generate these different knowledge-forms, and that these different forms constitute the conditions under which classes themselves develop. In other words, 'knowledges' are not merely produced *by* one or other class but rather they provide the very conditions under which classes may exist and develop. In particular, neither the service class nor deskilled white-collar workers could exist without what Sohn-Rethel calls the 'fetishism of intellectual labour' (1978, pp. 13–16) and the corresponding appropriation of knowledge away from directly productive labour. Hence, classes based on 'educated labour' do not merely generate particular contents of such knowledge. Rather the development of such classes transforms existing class relations because their very formation depends upon the possession of particular kinds of knowledge. And this means that that knowledge has been appropriated away from the direct producers. This appropriation, moreover, means that various knowledges are systematised in the form of different sciences and promulgated through education, and it is these processes which enable labour to be more effectively exploited as a routine, regular and systematic feature of capitalist relations. Furthermore, we shall seek to show that although some division between mental and manual labour is inscribed within the nature of generalised commodity relations, it does *not* follow that the 'fetishism of intellectual labour' and its heightened appropriation from manual labour is an automatic consequence of such relations.

The most systematic exploration of at least some of these issues is to be found in Sohn-Rethel (1978). He attempts to show that the conceptual basis for cognition, and especially for the intellectual labour which is involved in the pursuit of truth and the growth of natural science, is not a transcendental necessity as Kant had maintained. Rather it has to be related to the basic form of the 'social synthesis' characterising the epoch within which science materialises. Categories of thought are historical and social. What is the nature, then, of the social synthesis within which scientific thought becomes possible? Sohn-Rethel's answer lies in the form analysis of the nature of exchange and of abstract labour. He argues that there are parallels between the abstractions involved in exchange and the abstractions necessary for thought; that the social synthesis within which the former occurs produces the forms of thought premised upon the latter; and that these forms of thought are those socially, or functionally, necessary for reproducing the social synthesis. Sohn-Rethel thus sees himself as filling what is a major lacuna in Marx, namely, a theory of knowledge and hence of the division between mental and manual labour. It is moreover a politically crucial lacuna, for, without such a theory, and the resulting prescription to recombine mental and manual labour, one of the preconditions for a classless society remains unexplicated (p. 21).

Inherent in the process of commodity exchange is the force of abstraction, what Sohn-Rethel terms the exchange abstraction. This results from the division between use-value and exchange-value, from the fact that whenever commodity exchange takes place it does so in effective 'abstraction' from use (see p. 25, as well as the discussion in Kapferer, 1980, p. 77). The process of exchange is thus abstract although the consciousness of the agents involved is not (since people have to consider how they might use the commodities which are for sale). And this abstraction is particularly developed when one of the commodities being exchanged comes to serve as a means of exchange of all the others. (This role falls upon that commodity which is most durable, divisible and mobile; see Sohn-Rethel, 1978, p. 58.) The existence of money hence serves as the basis for a social synthesis whch is separate from the operations of man's material interchange with nature. Further, there is a conversion of the abstraction of exchange premissed upon money into the abstraction of intellectual labour. The real abstraction is converted into the conceptual abstraction since the former, being based on the minted coin, involves objectification of a material abstracted from use and viewed solely for exchange and to bear value.

Sohn-Rethel goes on to try to explain both the existence of the abstract, philosophical thought of the Greeks in terms of the domination of exchange-value within the ancient Greek communities (see Kapferer, 1980, pp. 78–81) and the crucial links between the growth of capitalist relations of production and of mathematics. In the latter he is concerned to ask how we acquired the intellectual capacity for our knowledge of nature that so far outstrips the knowledge which existed prior to the development of the division between mental and manual labour. Mathematics is central to this process because it is 'the only symbolic language that frees itself from human activity and the latter's actual performance (manual or otherwise)' (quoted in Kapferer, 1980, p. 83). Where there was a unity of head and hand, then labour could only take a practical form, and it could only be conceptualised through demonstration or everyday speech. Mathematics by contrast enables the conceptualisation of the system abstracted from our direct knowledge of it. And any part of nature can be formulated in theoretical terms whose relationships are specified mathematically. Sohn-Rethel characterises mathematics as 'the human mind in its socialised form' (1978, p. 130) and as such it directly mirrors money, it is money without its material attachments and hence is no longer recognisable as such but rather as 'pure intellect'.

Much of Sohn-Rethel's later discussion concerns the development of a 'plant economy' and hence of trends towards some re-socialisation of 'mental' and 'manual' labour within the 'third stage' of advanced capitalism. We shall not consider this here since there is no reason to believe that there is, in fact, a sufficiently strong contradiction between the 'plant' and 'market' economies that would re-socialise mental and manual labour as Sohn-Rethel believes (see Kapferer, 1980, pp. 94–5). What is important for us is his analysis of the changing forms of knowledge which are dependent upon the socialisation of unproductive labour. In particular, a crucial aspect of the growth of generalised commodity exchange is that of a socialised form of thought separate from the physical labour which is carried on independently by each producer. This socialised thought is that of mathematics, which enables the precise specification of the relationships between events in nature. The independence of these events parallels the independence of the relations of commodity exchange which comprise the new basis of the social synthesis.

There are, not surprisingly, many difficulties in Sohn-Rethel's argument and, in particular, he does not sufficiently clearly link together the growth of capitalist commodity relations with advances in the socialisation of intellectual thought. He also ignores the considerable variations in the institutional and class bases of intellectual thought within different capitalist societies and the effects that these have on the patterns of socialisation. These variations are reflected in the growth, both of science (and later of social science), and of formalised/systematised education. We shall consider both of these below. Before doing so, however, it is important to note two further aspects of intellectual knowledge. First, as Sohn-Rethel puts it: 'The contribution of the intellectual labourer is directly social labour. In proportion as it partakes of truth, the scientist's research is valid for all, and done on behalf of society as a whole' (quoted in Kapferer, 1980, p. 81). This presupposes a certain traffic in commodities so that the results of research are made available through face-to-face interchange, journals and books. But more important, because of the universalised character of the use-values of knowledge, specific groups will regulate access to such values and to their employment. The employment of credentials, generally guaranteed by the state, directly derives from the universalised character of the use-values of intellectual knowledge. We shall explore this further below. Secondly, Sohn-Rethel discusses intellectual labour as though it were uniformly distributed across all societies in which there is widespread commodity exchange. However, there are important spatial variations in the distribution of places within the socialised relations of unproductive labour. Once intellectual labour is socialised then it may be reorganised, re-located and recomposed, nationally and internationally, as a consequence of the relations both within and between different nation-states.

In general, Sohn-Rethel does not sufficiently explore certain transformations in the nature of capitalist production. We believe that it is necessary to distinguish between two basic forms of such relations: that of the socialisation of productive labour, and that of the socialisation of unproductive labour.

THE SOCIALISATION OF UNPRODUCTIVE LABOUR

We begin here by considering the distinctions drawn by Marx between the formal and the real subsumption of labour. Under the former, although labour appears to be put to work by capital, or objectified labour, there is no fundamental modification in the real nature of the labour process (see Marx, 1976, p. 1019). Capital subsumes labour as it is found; it takes over the existing labour process. The actual mode of working is not changed, and the only means of increasing surplus-value are either by working labour for longer hours, or by increasing the scale of operations (p. 1022). In each case capital does not intervene within the process of production itself.

By contrast, with the real subsumption of labour properly capitalist relations are established. There is the production of relative suplus-value through the direct subordination of labour to capital. The labour process is transformed and there is the gigantic development of the social forces of production. Marx summarises this process:

> The *social* productive forces of labour, or the productive forces of directly social, *socialised* (i.e. collective) labour, came into being through cooperation, division of labour within the workshop, the use of *machinery*, and in general the transformation of production by the conscious *use* of the sciences, of mechanics, chemistry, etc. for specific ends, technology, etc. and similarly, through the enormous increase of *scale* corresponding to such developments. This entire development of the productive forces of *socialised labour* (in contrast to the more or less isolated labour of individuals), and together with it the *use of science* (the *general* product of serial development), in the *immediate process of production*, takes the form of the *productive power of capital*. (Marx, 1976, p. 1024).

We can characterise these developments, including the tendency to '*multiply* and *diversify the spheres of production* and their sub-spheres' (p. 1037), as the 'socialisation of productive labour'. Now, although Marx devotes considerable attention to the distinction between productive and unproductive labour, he does not explore in any detail the further form of capital relations, namely, what we shall term the 'socialisation of unproductive labour'. It is well known that he considers that the category 'productive' does not merely refer to those engaged in purely manual labour. Products are the result of the combined labour of the collective aggregate worker; Marx says that some 'work better with their hands, others with their heads, one as a manager, engineer, technologist, etc., the other as overseer, the third as manual labourer or even drudge', (p. 1040). And there is a vast enlargement of organised knowledge, or science, which is necessary for augmenting the productive power of capital. Furthermore, there is an extensive process of capitalist incorporation, by which a 'whole mass of functions and activities which formerly had an aura of sanctity about them . . . (like all the professions . . .) . . . these became directly converted into *wage-labourers*' (p. 1042).

Marx thus refers to three developments, the collectivisation of labour, the growth of science (and more generally of knowledge and education), and the extension of wage-labour to unproductive workers. However, when he was writing it was not possible to see how these constituted a distinctive form of capitalist relations of production focused upon socialising, not productive labour, but unproductive labour. As we shall see, this involves not only the replacement of single capitalists by a complex managerial hierarchy (as in Carchedi's notion of global capital), but also the development of new forms of knowledge, accumulation, labour process and class relations. We will, though, initially and briefly, consider why such a distinctive form of capitalist relations develops.

There are four interdependent reasons for the 'socialisation of unproductive labour': (*a*) growth in working-class real wages and resultant transformation in its 'historically and morally' determined needs; (*b*) the large growth in so-called service employment and the relative, and in some cases absolute, decline in manufacturing employment; (*c*) the vast expansion in the size and complexity of the planning function attendant upon technological and ownership changes; and (*d*) the development of working-class and other popular struggles which necessitate new forms of management and supervision, and of an enlarged and grossly more complex state.

(*a*) There are a number of elements involved here: the growth in real wages and the decline in the obviously subsistence requirement within the reproduction of labour-power; the heightened demand for increasingly differentiated modes of consumer provision; the resulting increase in modes of product differentiation; the expansion in demand for and provision of educational and health services; the heightened demand for and commodification of culture, leisure and entertainments; and the increased need to use complex domestic equipment which needs to be invented, produced and serviced (see Mandel, 1975, pp. 390–5).

(*b*) It is characteristic of all the advanced capitalist economies that there is a rapid and sustained increase in 'service' employment so that by 1975 it exceeded manufacturing employment in all the West European countries except for West Germany and Luxembourg (see Marquand, 1980, p. 27). There are a number of factors which account for the increase of the service sector: the availability of large quantities of capital which can only be valorised outside manufacturing industry where the rate of profit has tended to fall (see Mandel, 1975, p. 389, as well as Heap, 1980); the increased need for markets so as to ensure the realisation of value (for example, market research); the extension of commodity production to new areas where most or all of the labour is 'mental' (for example, producing computer software); the increased embodiment of such mental labour within separate capital units providing 'producer services' for capital (for example, operations research; see Greenfield, 1966); the growth of new technology which permits the generation of new forms of use-value provision (for example, computer games); and the expansion of the state and the increasingly socialised forms by which labour-power is reproduced (for example, health care).

(*c*) A crucially relevant feature of contemporary capitalism is the reduction in the turnover-time of fixed capital, which results from, and contributes to, the acceleration of technological innovation (see Mandel, 1975, pp. 223ff.). Such innovations are crucial in enabling capital units to earn 'technological rents'. However, such rents are increasingly of a very short-term nature (the silicon chip industry, for instance) because of the extraordinary rise in the degree to which capital becomes obsolete. As a result there is both an increased speed with which old plant/machinery has to be replaced with new plant/machinery, and increased necessity for there to be general repairs which necessarily involve the continual updating of the existing technology. And these in turn imply, not only a huge jump in the cost of new capital investments (often going beyond the resources of a single capital unit), but a great increase in the periods necessary for experimentation and preparation for production. These result in a vast expansion in the attention that has to be devoted to planning within each capital unit, both of the exact forms of research, development and technology, and of the future markets for the commodities in question. Planning becomes absolutely essential to the processes of capitalist production and realisation. A growing division of labour can only be combined with the objective socialisation of the labour process if there is a substantial extension of the 'intermediate functions' of commerce, planning and the services (see Mandel, 1975, ch. 12; more generally here, see Bell, 1974, and Gershuny, 1978, for sharply contrasting views). Some of the growth in so-called 'services' hence consists in the development of producer services which are directly relevant to the sustaining of capitalist production relations (see Marquand, 1980, for the most accessible data).

(*d*) There are three important aspects of struggle relevant here: first, the general increase in the trade union/shop steward organisation of the labour force with the resulting effort by capital to devise compensating forms of managerial strategy often taking a national or international form; secondly, the expansion of the state in response to this 'challenge of labour' and the development of relatively non-commodified forms of reproducing labour-power; and thirdly, the growth of a wide variety of movements and struggles dependent upon the shift towards the dominance of the 'sphere of reproduction' within civil society (see Urry, 1981b, ch. 8).

So far we can see that the socialisation of unproductive labour stems from a number of transformations: within the sphere of circulation (increased real wages); within the sphere of production (centralisation, internationalisation and transformed technology); within civil society (changed 'needs' and struggles); and within the state (resulting from different social struggles). Furthermore, because there are these different elements involved, it cannot be presumed that the degree and forms of socialisation are functionally best-suited to the particular accumulation requirements of the given capitalist economy.

There are three main forms taken by such socialised unproductive labour: (1) the social relations involved in organising and managing the productive labour engaged in producing materially tangible commodities; (2) the social relations involved in organising, managing and producing predominantly intangible commodities which are directly exchanged with revenue; and (3) the social relations involved in organising, managing and producing intangible commodities which realise surplus-value for the owners of capital.

Our argument is that these constitute a set of social relations which are, from the viewpoint of the system as a whole, unproductive. They represent a net deduction from capital. However, at the same time they may be productive judged from the viewpoint of a single capital unit. This is to return to the distinction made in *Capital*, Vol. 2 (but not in *Theories of Surplus-Value*), where Marx distinguishes labour productive for capital as a whole from that which is productive for the individual capitalist (see Marx, 1978, pp. 209–11). This is clearly a crucial distinction in the analysis of the contemporary economy, as compared with the time when Marx was writing. In *Capital*, Vol. 1, he said that the 'types of work that are consumed as services and not in products separable from the worker and hence not capable of existing as commodities independently of him, but which are yet capable of being directly exploited in *capitalist* terms, are of microscopic significance when compared with the mass of capitalist production' (Marx, 1976, pp. 1044–5). As a result they 'may be entirely neglected' (p. 1045). However, they cannot be neglected in contemporary capitalist societies. From the viewpoint of social capital as a whole there is an enormous deduction of expenditure devoted to socialised unproductive labour.

Moreover, contrary to Carchedi, we do not view the function of this labour as purely that of supervision and management (see above, pp. 63–4). Other aspects of their labour involve the conversion of money into commodities and commodities into money, implementing and monitoring technical developments, reproducing labour-power, producing intangible luxury products, and so on. Furthermore, again contrary to Carchedi, it is not the case that this labour is necessarily organised in a complex hierarchical structure; it will often be located within small capital units. The most important issue, though, concerns the social relations which connect together these different components of unproductive labour. Unlike the stage of early capitalist relations, when unproductive labour was organised personally or on a relatively small scale, with capitalists directly managing or organising labour or providing unproductive services, in the later form there are highly complex interdependencies between these different elements of unproductive labour which is organised in terms of particular relations between different places within a wide range of unproductive activities (see Hirst, 1979, p. 47). There are a number of points to note about the places consequently produced.

(1)   They may be fragmented and incumbents will not necessarily effect personal control over productive labour. Such control will, if achieved, result from the reproduction of the social relations between places.

(2)   Because of the socialisation of much labour the reproduction of capitalist relations in this later stage is thus far less dependent upon the specific motivations of particular capitalists or of the service class or of deskilled white-collar workers (see Abercrombie, *et al.*, 1980, ch. 6).

(3)   There is no direct connection between the functions of capital and labour, on the one hand, and the divisions within the labour force between skilled/unskilled, mental/manual and managerial/non-managerial, on the other (see Hirst, 1979, pp. 48–9); the former does not directly generate distinctions within the latter.

(4)   Many of the places produced within the sphere of unproductive labour require various kinds and levels of 'educated labour'. This has to be reproduced like any other socialised labour, that is, in large quantities and categorised in terms of objective means of assessment.

In the following section we shall consider in detail the last two points, through analysing the relationship of education and of educated labour to the division between capital and labour.

THE DEVELOPMENT OF EDUCATED LABOUR

In 1824 W. Thompson made the following perceptive observation:

The man of knowledge and the productive labourer came to be widely divided from each other, and knowledge, instead of remaining the handmaid of labour in the hand of the labourer . . . has almost everywhere arrayed itself against labour systematically deluding and leading them astray in order to render their muscular power entirely mechanical and obedient. (Quoted in Rosenberg, 1981, p. 22).

In the rest of this chapter we shall try to show: first, that the establishment of this contradiction between knowledge and manual labour was a matter of struggle and did not directly follow from the accumulation requirements of the growing capitalist economy; secondly, that this struggle put labour and its representatives in a singular contradiction since it both benefited from, and was disadvantaged by, the growth of general educational qualifications (as opposed to those which are firm/industry-specific); and thirdly, these various struggles produced considerable variation in the salience of the boundaries, in the size, and in the economic and political significance of 'educated labour', that is, in the degree to which the middle classes function as 'organic intellectuals' of the capitalist class.

First, then, we shall argue that the separation of mental and manual labour does not follow directly from the development of industry, or from the nature of technology, or from the growth of capitalist relations *per se*. And with regard to the views of Sohn-Rethel we would argue that widespread commodity relations provide only a necessary condition for the socialisation of mental labour. What are the other conditions under which this socialisation is realised?

It is now often noted that the growth of the factory had very profound effects in changing people's work habits and experience. There was some shift from an orientation to task towards an orientation to time (see Thompson, 1967). However, well after the development of the factory, much of the discipline and control of the workers was often left to a semi-independent third party – inside contractors. This was particularly important in the USA in the 1860s and 1870s – it was an arrangement whereby the contractors hired and fired their own employees, set their wages, disciplined them and determined what production methods should be followed (see Clawson, 1980, ch. 3; Stark, 1980, p. 100; and Littler, 1982, ch. 6 on Britain). Elsewhere there was a system of 'indirect control' which persisted into the twentieth century, with either foremen or skilled workers organising much of the labour process (see Nelson, 1975, ch. 3 on 'The Foreman's Empire'). It was a premiss of all these systems that workers knew more than anyone else about how to do their work and they would therefore retain control of the details of the labour process. The growth in the factory did not therefore result in a necessary increase in the social control that capital could exercise over labour; the real subsumption of the labourer was not simply brought about by the factory system (but for a contrary view, see Marglin, 1974, as well as the discussion in Hill, 1981, ch. 2). For this to occur and hence for the development of a large-scale industrial bureaucracy, two particular forms of resistance had to be overcome: first, from the workforce themselves who had always been, in part at least, in control of their own labour; and secondly, from capitalists and existing managers who believed that a growth in 'scientific' management was an unnecessary and dangerous expense which would undermine their own prerogatives (see Nelson, 1975, pp. 75–6; Clawson, 1980, pp. 68–9, especially on Adam Smith's criticism of managers; Stark, 1980, p. 91). In other words, the growth of a large socialised sphere of unproductive labour was not a necessary consequence of increased size but depended upon specific struggles in order to overcome these forms of resistance (although see Edwards, 1979, pp. 85–8, who mainly employs a 'size' explanation). In particular, it is necessary to explain the particular pattern of unproductive labour that developed – since what might have happened was the more or less proportionate expansion in the number of 'direct controllers' where much of the 'knowledge' of production was left in the heads and hands of the direct producers. That this did not occur can be attributed to the particular conditions of struggle in early twentieth-century USA: namely, the growing strength of the working-class movement, especially from the 1894 Pullman strike up to the 'holocaust' of 1919 (on the 'control' struggles of 1901–4, 1916–20, see Edwards, 1979, pp. 49–50; Montgomery, 1979, pp. 98–101); the growing concentration and centralisation of capital especially as the declining rate of profit made itself felt from the 1880s onwards (see R. Nelson, 1959; Williamson, 1974; Edwards, 1979, ch. 3); and the growth of reformist movements of intellectuals and professionals which in part legitimated the 'scientisation' of labour (see Edwards, 1979, pp. 48–9). These provided the context within which the Taylorist strategy for capital emerged (see Taylor, 1947). Taylor acknowledged that it was inherent in the labour process for workers to control the details of their work. Thus, as long as workers knew more than their managers, then management would have to persuade the workers to co-operation. This could be clearly seen in relationship to piecework – since management did not know how long in fact it took to do each piece of work, it was rational for workers to engage in 'systematic soldiering' and hence to restrict output. Taylor realised that the only long-term solution to this from the viewpoint of capital was to devise a new system of capitalist control that would overcome the rational tendency for workers to restrict output (see Burawoy, 1979, pp. 79–81, though, on modern management's collusion or even active involvement in such restrictions). And this could only be achieved by transforming the very form of knowledge possessed by workers. In particular, it would be necessary to create the separate category of 'management', which had until then enjoyed only a somewhat protean existence.

The first stage in this process was for the management to learn what its workers already knew. 'The Managers assume . . . the burden of gathering together all of the traditional knowledge, which in the past has been possessed by the workmen' (Taylor, 1947, p. 36; see Littler, 1978, more generally here). The second stage was for the management to 'take over all of the work for which they are better fitted than the workman; almost every act of the workman should be preceded by various preparatory acts' of the management (p. 38). As a result there was a vast growth in the bureaucratisation of industry since Taylor advocated the creation of a 'planning room' where there should be a concentration of the 'brain-work' which had been removed from the shop floor. Thus in the third stage of the process, management had to specify in advance precisely what each worker was required to do. And, although these tasks may have been similar to those which had been done previously, they were now to be determined within the 'planning room', or more generally within the bureaucratic structure. Taylor refers to the almost equal division of the actual work of the establishment between the workman, on the one hand, and the management, on the other. Under the old system, practically the whole problem was left to the workman, while under scientific management there were two divisions, and one of these divisions was deliberately handed over to the side of the management (see pp. 38f.). The Taylor system, then, involved an enormous expansion in what he himself called 'non-producers'. At the same time he advocated increases in the detail division of labour, speed-ups and various technical changes (see Braverman, 1974; Burawoy, 1978; and many others).

There is great controversy as to the degree to which Taylorian scientific management was implemented. However, we are not here concerned directly with the degree to which Taylor is responsible for the changes introduced or whether in practice there were major modifications effected in 'scientific management' (on these issues, see especially Nelson, 1974; Braverman, 1974; Edwards, 1979; Littler, 1982). Montgomery convincingly shows that the following basic principles of scientific management were generally implemented in American industry by the mid to late 1920s: the centralised planning and integrating of the successive stages of production; the systematic analysis of each distinct operation; the detailed instruction and supervision of each worker in the performance of each discrete task; and the designing of wage payments to induce workers to do what they were told (1979, ch. 5). This growth in the bureaucratisation of the control function in industry and of 'educated labour' was not the consequence of technological imperatives, nor simply of size (for such an interpretation, see the otherwise informative Chandler, 1977), but stemmed from the historically specific process of class struggle in the early years of this century, particularly during and just after the First World War (see Stark, 1980, pp. 107–114; Montgomery, 1979, ch. 5). Moreover, it was not a development which attenuated that struggle, but rather it transformed its parameters. The socialisation of unproductive labour and the development of a mass of 'educated labour' introduced new forms in which struggles materialised. These increasingly revolved around the 'professionalisation' of business and 'progressive' reforms; the growth in science and knowledge and the attack on the skilled crafts; and the importance of expanding access to education and the obtaining of educational credentials (on Taylorism and Progressivism, see Haber, 1964).

One pertinent indicator of these developments in the USA was the extraordinary expansion in higher education between 1880 and 1930, by contrast both with that of the earlier period and that of the other leading capitalist nations. By 1930 the USA possessed more institutions of higher education than France possessed academic personnel and its university and college population was ten times larger than the secondary school population in France (see Debray, 1981, pp. 43–4; Mulhern, 1981, p. 49; the population in the USA was only three times that of France in 1930). Incidentally, this failure to expand higher education in France before the 1930s and 1940s was related to the retarded development of the new middle class that we noted in Chapter 4 above. It would also seem plausible to suggest that this especially large increase in both the size of the middle classes and of the mobility into them in the USA (their proportion increased from 12 to 22 per cent between 1900 and 1930; see Kocka, 1980, p. 19) was an important factor in preventing the development of strong work, market and political divisions between such employees and the working class in this period. Kocka talks of the 'indistinctness and relative insignificance of the collar line in industry' (1980, p. 117 and *passim*), although it should be noted that he attributes this to the lack of bureaucratic and corporatist structures in pre-industrial America (compared particularly with Germany up to 1933).

This early growth of 'educated labour' in the USA shows that it is important not to overemphasise the similarities between different capitalist societies (see Littler, 1982, on the Ambrit fallacy). In the USA there are five distinctive features to note: the early development of the division between mental and manual labour; the organisation of mental labour within large industrial bureaucracies; the lack of strong work, market and status divisions between deskilled white-collar workers and the working class; the early importance of professional rather than bureaucratic organisations as the basis for group mobilisations (see Kocka, 1980, pp. 141–53); and the domination of the world economy which thus meant that a higher proportion of mental labourer functions were located in the USA.

In the following section we shall amplify these specific points and try to show more systematically the relationship of educational credentials to the development of middle-class labour.

CAPITALISM AND CREDENTIALS

It is erroneous to suggest that the nature of educational credentials perfectly mirrors the requirements of the capitalist economy. Mediating between such credentials and capitalist relations of production is civil society in general, and the market for different kinds of labour-power in particular. This means that various social groupings will control access to particular places within the social division of labour, in particular by struggling to sustain or enlarge the educational credentials necessary for such access. There will be a tendency for such credentials to be hierarchically structured and for social groupings to try to specify credentials progressively farther up this hierarchy. It will generally be in a grouping's interest to effect a degree of social closure by sustaining the claim that their labour is predominantly mental and hence access to it requires specific educational credentials. The existence of such hierarchically organised credentials has a number of critical consequences.

(1) Non-possessors of a given credential will be generally denied access to particular places within the social division of labour.

(2) Possessors of the credential will not necessarily gain access to these places, and, even if they do, they will probably not directly use the 'knowledge' so gained (see Berg, 1970); such credentials are chiefly important for what they indicate about one's motivation, loyalty and commitment to particular values.

(3) Such credentials locate individual possessors within a hierarchy and this effects the distribution of individuals to places (see the discussion of this in Hussain, 1976, pp. 419–20).

(4) There is no one-to-one relationship between credentials and places – this relationship varies both within and between societies; credentials are important in determining one's port of entry into the internal labour market (see below, p. 111); there is, however, a general tendency for the credentials required for particular places progressively to increase; hence the phenomena of 'qualification-escalation', exam-oriented learning and the 'diploma disease' (see Berg, 1970; Braverman, 1974; Dore, 1976).

However, these observations on the relationship between capitalism and credentialism have not been satisfactorily integrated with an analysis of social classes. Three texts in which interesting connections have been made are Poulantzas, 1973, Ehrenreich and Ehrenreich, 1979a, and Stewart, Prandy and Blackburn, 1980. However, in each case only one aspect is considered in detail: in Poulantzas, the effects of the mental/manual division, and the celebration of the former, on class formation; in the Ehrenreichs, how the specific market capacity of a college education generates the professional-managerial class; and in Stewart *et al.*, the importance of qualifications for the occupational and social mobility of 'clerks'. We will now try to construct a more systematic analysis which incorporates certain of these insights.

First of all, we should distinguish between three kinds of qualification:

(a) *everyone's qualifications*, in particular literacy and numeracy (albeit divided by sex, age and race);

(b) *general qualifications* obtained through education and certified through national diplomas;

(c) *corporation or occupation-specific qualifications* which are relatively non-transferable (this is a modification of Sengenberger, 1978; and see Kreckel, 1980).

Sengenberger argues that in contemporary large corporations there is a tendential polarisation between *a* and *c*, with a general devaluation of *b*. However, although the general tendencies towards deskilling will generate such polarisation, what is remarkable is the vast expansion of *b* in all the major capitalist countries although, as we have already noted, with considerable variation between societies (France/USA), and over time (more likely during periods of economic expansion). What are the reasons for the growth of *b* – a growth in the hierarchisation of mental labour which does not directly mirror capitalist relations of production?

The first reason for the expansion of *b* is that it represents a socialisation of the costs of training and hence would prove attractive to individual capital-units especially at times of economic restructuring. This becomes of increasing importance as the division of mental and manual work proceeds and the potential costs of on-the-job training get ever more enlarged (see Hales, 1980, on some aspects of this). Secondly, the increased power of the popular classes becomes focused upon expanding access to education, which is taken to provide an increasingly important means of individual mobility. Indeed, the growth of general qualifications (as opposed to *c*) represents a substantial labour market gain for the popular classes (since credential-holders are not tied to particular employers). Thirdly, the very universality of mental knowledge appropriated from the direct producers is the precondition for, and the result of, the growth of various forms of higher education – such forms will generate general qualifications as opposed to those which are corporation- or occupation-specific. Indeed one clear precondition of *b* is the prior existence of universities and their ability to augment their power at a time when it might have been thought that expanding capitalist relations would have generated highly vocational training providing mostly qualifications of type *c* (see Rothblatt, 1968, on the modest late nineteenth-century reforms in Cambridge). Fourthly, part of the pressure for general educational qualifications comes from the 'service class' within the late Victorian period, who struggled both to undermine the power of the landed and capitalist classes over recruitment (through the family enterprise, into particular state institutions, etc.) and to prevent the potential upward mobility of children of the popular classes (see Henderson, 1976, on the use of IQ tests with respect to the latter, as well as the more general Williams, 1961). Fifthly, the socialisation of unproductive labour, or what Hales calls the Taylorisation of intellectual work, necessitates a 'reserve army' of mental labourers – and it is a precondition of such an army that they can be easily brought into, and expelled from, the labour market. This presupposes the existence of general qualifications independent of specific employers. And finally, the extension of state employment involves the increased use of general qualifications provided within the partially state-financed education system.

Thus far we have seen that the development of capitalist relations will customarily involve an extension in the use of general qualifications, provided especially through the education system. This, we have suggested, is not a technical necessity but follows from developments within capital, labour and the state. At the same time, capitalism involves, in its later stage, the socialisation of unproductive labour. There is an increasingly symbiotic relationship between the two processes. One crucial consequence of this symbiosis is that the places generated by the socialisation of unproductive labour are increasingly differentiated in terms of the patterns by which educational credentials are hierarchised. We shall discuss certain aspects of this process in the next chapter.

7
Middle Class or Service Class?

In the last chapter we discussed certain underlying processes in the development of capitalism, especially the socialisation of unproductive labour and the related issue of the organisation of knowledge and the middle classes. In this chapter we have to take further an analysis of the constitution of a class or classes lying between capital and labour, an analysis which we shall in turn relate to the importance of educational credentials in distinguishing between class places within contemporary capitalism. Our aim will be to distinguish sharply between the service class and deskilled white-collar workers in terms of the market and work situations of their respective class places. Before doing so, however, we must clarify the distinction between places and persons that we will employ.

PERSONS AND PLACES

The distinction between persons and places is one that is made in much recent social theory. We now discuss two views, both of which advocate a radical distinction between persons and places but which have very different theoretical implications. Poulantzas puts the issue particularly clearly. For him classes are 'groupings of social agents, defined principally but not exclusively by their place in the production processes, i.e. in the economic sphere' (1975, p. 14). Further,

> The principal aspect of an analysis of social classes is that of their places in the class struggle, it is not that of the agents that compose them. Social classes are not empirical groups of individuals, social groups, that are 'composed' by simple addition; the relations of these agents among themselves are thus not inter-personal relations. The class membership of the various agents depends on the class places that they occupy: it is moreover distinct from the class origin, the social origin, of the agents. (1975, p. 17)

The choice of the word 'agent' (for which we substitute 'person') is clearly no accident. Poulantzas wants to ascribe a certain passivity to the human individual. Agents are merely those elements that bear the functions that attach to class places largely defined in terms of economic practices (as we saw, in effect, in Chapter 5 above). Therefore, although classes are seen as being groups of individuals, these individuals are functionaries and consequently class analysis amounts to the analysis of places within the social division of labour.

This point of view is seen clearly in Poulantzas' account of the reproduction of class places, and the reproduction and distribution of agents into these places. The second of these is, in Poulantzas' view, subordinate to the first. While it is true that agents do have to be trained to fill places, it is equally true that the distribution of agents does not depend on their own intentions or qualifications but on the reproduction of the places themselves. Similarly, the mobility of agents between places does not have any implications for the analysis of class. As Poulantzas says:

> However, it is clear that, even on the absurd assumption that from one day to the next, or even from one generation to the next, the bourgeoisie would take all the places of workers and vice versa, nothing fundamental about capitalism would be changed since the places of bourgeoisie and proletariat would still be there, and this is the principal aspect of the reproduction of capitalist relations. (1975, p. 33)

A view in many respects the reverse of that adopted by Poulantzas is advanced by Stewart *et al.* (1980). They do not employ the terminology of agents, or persons and places, but their use of 'incumbent' and 'job' carries much the same meaning. For them, classes are constituted by aggregates of individuals who happen to be employed in various occupations which can be defined in terms of work tasks. However, it is essential to distinguish workers from the work they perform because, over their careers, people will not always have the same occupation. One can no longer equate individuals with jobs and, consequently, since classes are composed of individuals, one cannot use job or occupation as the basis of class determination. These general arguments about the relationship between job and incumbent are based on an investigation of the occupation of clerks, the details of which we discussed in Chapter 3. Stewart *et al.* argue that male clerks have a high chance of upward mobility if they enter as clerks fairly young, making it particularly difficult to identify clerical work with clerks. Hence, we cannot refer to the class position of clerks in terms of clerical work because the class origins and destinations of clerks are so very diverse.

Stewart *et al.* are, therefore, radical in demoting the significance of occupation or place which cannot, in their view, be the basis for a definition of class. Their general argument is, however, narrowly founded: first, because it is based on the significance of mobility; and secondly, because it is based on a study of clerks. That is, they only want to minimise the salience of occupation because of the chances of occupational mobility. 'If, indeed, promotion out of clerical work were rare, the use-fulness of the category as a description of stratification arrangements would be greatly enhanced' (p. 153). However, we have already argued that such promotion out of clerical work is not nearly so common as Stewart *et al.* think. More important still, the mobility experience of male clerks is not typical of male workers as a whole, as the Nuffield mobility study shows. In sum, one cannot undermine the salience of occupation from evidence of the mobility experience of clerks. Further, as Stewart *et al.* show in their discussion of the reproduction of classes, it is very diffi-cult analytically to separate discussion of the qualities of places from that of the aggregate of persons occupying them.

In rejecting a radical distinction between persons and places, which has the effect of reducing the salience of place, we wish to conceptualise classes as systems of places. It is important to stress that classes are not simply aggregates of places; an analysis of the social relations between places is essential for an adequate understanding of class. However, in our view, Poulantzas is incorrect in seeing the characteristics of persons as being irrelevant to the analysis of classes. Thus, although classes are constituted as places, class practices are partly determined by the charac-teristics of persons who fill those places, characteristics determined by a number of determinants outside class places. There is, therefore, an inter-action between places and persons, class and class practices. This view is closely bound up with our arguments in favour of a realist theory of class and we shall return to the point in Chapter 8. We shall treat class places as elements of real entities – classes – while the causal powers of those enti-ties are actuated, among other things, by the manner in which people are recruited to the places, in other words, by the processes of class forma-tion.

Although in our discussion of the views of Stewart *et al.* we treated occupation and place as more or less synonymous, this equation can be misleading. That is, although occupational designations are very often used as a convenient shorthand for class position, they are not theoretic-ally equivalent. Occupation typically refers primarily to sets of job tasks, that is, it refers to positions within the technical division of labour. The concept of place, on the other hand, and hence the concept of class, refers primarily to the social relations at work, or positions within the social division of labour. Occupation, largely based on technical aspects of the labour process, and place, largely based on social relations within a labour process, are therefore different kinds of concept, even if, in certain circumstances, it is permissible to use one as a shorthand for the other. Furthermore, occupational designations may actually obscure class positions because technical features do not entail social features. One aspect of this concerns the frequently made claim explored in Chapter 3, that the class structure has become very much more complex and hence class divisions can no longer be established easily. In a sense this is true because differentiations within the technical division of labour may have produced occupational differentiation. It follows from our earlier argument, however, that this does not necessarily mean class differentiation.

So far, we have identified classes as constituted by places and places as being constituted by social relations of the labour process, not by occupation. We now attempt to make this designation more precise.

MARKET AND WORK SITUATIONS

Our position will be that 'places' are characterised by distinctive market and work situations.

The concepts of market and work situation, although they derive ultimately from the writings of Weber, were introduced into British sociology by Lockwood. Market situation refers to 'the economic position narrowly conceived, consisting of source and size of income, degree of job security, and opportunity for upward social mobility'. Both together make up class position. Work situation comprises 'The set of social relationships in which the individual is involved at work by virtue of his position in the division of labour' (Lockwood, 1958, p. 15). In Lockwood's view the clerk has both a better market situation and an advantageous work situation when compared with manual workers. Even if the market situation were similar, differences in work situation would be enough to place the clerk in a different class position. Indeed, in a crucially important sense, Lockwood believes that the work situation is a more fundamental determinant than market situation. 'Without doubt in modern industrial society, the most important social conditions shaping the psychology of the individual are those arising out of the organisation of production, administration and distribution. In other words, the work situation' (p. 208).

It should be noted that Lockwood's concepts of market and work situation are concepts of place (or occupation, a reasonable shorthand), not person. That is, they describe characteristics of occupations, not the people recruited to those occupations. It is not clear whether Lockwood believes that clerks 'take on' the market and work situations of the places they occupy, but the effect of his position is that market and work situations define class because they are concepts of place. It should also be emphasised that Lockwood's account, and those of many Weberian writers who have followed his example, do not rely solely on characteristics of the market for labour, as some Marxists claim, but rather stress the dominance of work situation (what Marxists term the 'labour process').

Lockwood's discussion raises a number of issues, including what relation the work situation has to the concept of relations of production and, most important, what relationship, if any, obtains between market and work situation. Some light is thrown on these questions by the recent literature on labour markets which, we believe, establishes the primary importance of work situation. Kreckel (1980), for example, argues that the sociology of social stratification would benefit greatly from closer contact with labour market economics. His primary aim is the investigation of 'structural social inequality' by which he means the 'unequal distribution of possibilities of access to certain material and symbolic conditions' (p. 528). Mostly, in capitalist societies, access is dependent on position in the occupational opportunity structure, such positions being principally allocated through the labour market. People do not have equal bargaining power in the market, there being two main sources of asymmetry. The first, and more important, is the asymmetry between capital and labour, capital inevitably having the upper hand. However, there are also inequalities between various sectors of labour and these are the most significant sources of the structural social inequality mentioned earlier. If occupational positions are monopolised by a small number of occupants, bargaining strength is improved. This process of exclusion is usually known as social closure (see also Parkin, 1979). It is these inequalities in the labour market that are the chief focus of attention of recent work in labour market economics. Within this form of analysis there are various ways of characterising different segments of the labour market which may be fruitful in analysing occupational differentiation. Kreckel's argument is that from the various studies of labour markets, one can generate a set of concepts describing bargaining strength in capitalist labour markets, which are simultaneously concepts of social inequality.

In Kreckel's account, therefore, there is a direct connection between the analysis of markets and the notion of inequality, which is traditionally handled in sociology by the concept of class. At a number of points, however, his views create difficulties or require expansion. First, he studiously avoids referring to the term 'class' and it is, therefore, arguable that he misses an opportunity of relating to traditional accounts of the way that inequality is organised. This omission is especially baffling since Kreckel argues that the primary asymmetry in the labour market is between capital and labour. He does not develop this point and consequently it is difficult to know what the joint relationship of primary and secondary asymmetries is to social inequality. Secondly, Kreckel does not treat as problematic the matching of training and qualification to the actual skills required in any particular job. We made a similar point in the discussion of Giddens's concept of market capacity in Chapter 2. Giddens defines the 'new middle class' in terms of the educational and technical qualifications possessed by individuals. As we showed in Chapter 6, it is possible, however, that the skills required for white-collar jobs are such that qualifications are simply not appropriate. Some authors have suggested that there is a systematic mismatch between the demand for, and supply of, skills. Dore (1976) argues that there is a process of 'educational inflation' whereby the increased educational level of the workforce forces the employer to demand higher qualifications. Education becomes certification. Dore traces the transition from a system of apprenticeship to one of pre-career qualification in the civil engineering profession. Until 1897 no written examination of any kind was required for membership of the institution, just evidence of work done on the job. Gradually, however, qualifying examinations became necessary, until by 1970 a degree was a precondition for a professional career as an engineer. Dore is, however, certain that the increased importance of pre-career qualification is not related to an increased need for theoretical knowledge on the job. Among other things, it is not clear how theoretical knowledge is best concentrated into a period of three or four years at the beginning of a career or how someone can practise these early skills for a lifetime without any formal requirement to acquire new theoretical skills. Qualification is rather more of a gate than a training and relevant skills are learnt on the job. If this is true even of a 'practical' subject like civil engineering, it is even more likely to be true of the very many relatively unspecialised white-collar jobs for which qualifications are demanded. Of course, it may well be the case that occupations will vary in the degree to which qualifications match the objective job description and the objective job description matches the actual skills used.

Unfortunately, little is known about the skills required in white-collar occupations. Although not directly relevant to white-collar employment, the study by Blackburn and Mann entitled *The Working Class in the Labour Market* (1979) is helpful in this discussion. First, they show that few skills are actually employed. In fact, jobs which involved driving were ranked by their method, which depended on investigation of the technical work tasks, higher than most other jobs. This implies that a large proportion of the working population routinely use a skill in their everyday life in excess of those they use in their jobs. Secondly, most workers that they studied were objectively capable of acquiring the skills necessary for most of the jobs. Although management did indeed emphasise the importance of skill in internal promotion, on investigation they turned out to be concerned rather about worker co-operation.

> Responsibility, stability, trustworthiness – such are the qualities by which (reasonably enough) they wish to select and promote. From the employer's point of view, the internal labour market allows workers to demonstrate these qualities (if they have them) over a number of years before they reach jobs where mistakes would matter. (p. 280)

This last point suggests a third comment on Kreckel's position. If 'The internal labour market is fundamentally an apprenticeship in co-operation' (Blackburn and Mann, 1979, p. 108), the strong implication is that the traditional concepts of market and work situation are not independent and Lockwood's view that work situation is dominant takes on a definite plausibility. Similar implications flow from Edwards's study, *Contested Terrain* (1979). Edwards argues that the market for labour is not a unified whole but is segmented into three distinct parts – the secondary, subordinate primary and independent primary markets. The first of these contains:

> Low-paying jobs of casual labour, jobs that provide little employment security or stability and for which the links between one job a worker may hold and the next are slight. These are dead-end jobs offering little opportunity for advancement, requiring few skills, and promoting relatively high voluntary turnover. Neither security nor education seems to pay off. And since employers have little investment in matching workers and their jobs, they feel free to replace or dismiss workers as their labour needs change. (p. 170)

In contrast to the secondary jobs, primary jobs have some security with fairly stable employment, higher wages and some sort of link between successive jobs that a worker may hold. Subordinate and independent primary jobs differ from one another along a number of dimensions. Subordinate jobs, which include 'traditional' working-class occupations, are characterised by repetitive, routinised and machine-paced work tasks, relatively little skill and the presence of active unions. Independent primary jobs, by contrast,

> typically involve general, rather than firm specific skills; they may have career ladders that imply movements between firms; they are not centred on operating machinery; they typically require skills obtained in advanced or specialised schooling; they often demand educational credentials; they are likely to have occupational or professional standards for performance; and they are likely to require independent initiative or self-pacing. (p. 174)

Three main groups comprise the independent primary sector: middle management, workers with craft skills, and professionals.

From our point of view, the crucial point in Edwards's argument is that this labour market segmentation does not derive from the market itself. Unless either workers or employers have a high degree of market-power, which is unlikely, 'labour markets constitute a means of mediation; they reflect the underlying forces in production and in the labouring population' (p. 177). More specifically, each segment of the labour market is related to a particular form of control in the workplace. The secondary labour market is the market expression of workplaces organised by simple control, the subordinate primary market represents technical control, and the independent primary sector depends on bureaucratic control.

On Edwards's account, therefore, labour markets are the expression of work situation. However, this may be a little overstated since, as Penn (1982) argues, employers do not choose a particular technology because they wish to employ a particular system of control. This choice may also be partly dictated by technical requirements (see also Loveridge and Mok, 1979, pp. 131–3). Secondly, although Edwards sees managers as uniquely in control, actually workers, particularly through their unions, are also able to control certain aspects of their labour; there is a 'frontier of control' (see Goodrich, 1920). We conclude that work and market situations are interdependent concepts with the work situation as dominant. They cannot be treated as separate criteria of class position.

THE MARKET AND WORK SITUATION OF MIDDLE-CLASS PLACES: DESKILLED WHITE-COLLAR WORKERS

So far we have defined social classes as places constituted by a particular market and work situation. That which is often conventionally designated as the middle class in reality consists of two relatively discrete sets of market and work situations. The situation of deskilled white-collar workers is a great deal closer to that of the working class than it is to that of the 'upper'-middle class.

We have already reviewed some of the evidence concerning the market situation of deskilled white-collar workers (see Chapter 3). Further data are presented in Table 7.1.

Table 7.1   *Average Earnings in Pounds Sterling, Various Years 1935/6 to 1978*

Men	1935/6	1960	1970	1978
Higher professional	634	2,034	2,928	8,286
Lower professional	308	847	1,885	5,435
Managers	440	1,850	3,400	8,050
Clerks	192	682	1,337	3,701
Skilled	195	796	1,440	4,354
Unskilled	129	535	1,154	3,390
Women	1935/6	1960	1970	1978
Higher professional	—	—	2,460	6,712
Lower professional	211	606	1,224	3,872
Managers	—	1,000	1,870	5,070
Clerks	99	427	839	2,730
Skilled	86	395	677	2,246
Unskilled	73	285	610	2,275

Source: Adapted from Routh, 1980, pp. 120–1.

If one takes the relationship between the earnings of male clerks and those of unskilled male workers, the gap in earnings has narrowed over the years, until it approached parity in 1978. There has been a similar narrowing in differentials for the same two groups of women workers, although the gap is wider than it is for men. The earnings differential between clerks and managers has remained fairly constant, except that women clerks have improved their position relative to managers during the 1970s. This represents some rather crude evidence of the relative worsening in the earnings of clerks. Westergaard and Resler (1975) argue much more definitely that clerks (male) have dropped from a position of parity with skilled workers to a point well below the overall average, midway between the skilled and the semi-skilled. This is not the result of a general equalisation, either; it is rather a proletarianisation of some white-collar workers.

> The position especially of low-grade office and sales employees as workers who live by the sale of their labour power has been accentuated ... by the loss of the wage advantage from which they previously benefited by comparison with non-skilled manual labour. In terms of earnings, the gap has opened up wide between 'small' white-collar workers and the managers, administrators and 'established' professionals at the top of the tree – whose recorded earnings understate their total incomes, and whose at least partial control over their own terms and conditions of work puts them outside the market in which rank-and-file earners sell their labour. (pp. 75–6)

As we saw in Chapter 3, recent attention has concentrated on the promotion prospects of clerks which, if they were significant, would constitute an important part of the market situation of clerical workers. Stewart *et al.* (1980) use their findings to make some devastating criticisms of traditional accounts of clerical career patterns (see also Goldthorpe, 1980b, pp. 258–9). For example, Lockwood had suggested that the status of a white-collar job was one of the reasons why clerks took such apparently ill-rewarded work. However, Stewart *et al.* show that there is no need to rely on such an explanation for, given the relatively favourable promotion prospects of clerks, their future market situation is a good deal rosier than their present one. However, we would argue that it is not so clear that the promotion prospects of clerks in general are that good. Stewart *et al.* show clearly that the occupational destinations of clerks are indeed various. At age 30, of all male clerks 26 per cent will become manual workers, 14 per cent will stay as clerks and 60 per cent go to other non-manual work. However, not all the 60 per cent 'other non-manual' will represent promotion, although Stewart *et al.* explicitly state that it does, because 'clerk' is the lowest paid white-collar category. Furthermore, in common with many other studies of mobility, Stewart *et al.* do not consider the mobility chances of women. This omission is vitally important in an occupation in which some three-quarters of the workers are women (for more general discussion see Hindess, 1981). Little is known about the promotion prospects of female deskilled white-collar workers, but it is not an unreasonable assumption that they are relatively poor (but see Heath, 1981, ch. 4, as well as pp. 39–40 above). Taking all clerks together, men and women, prospects for advancement are not, therefore, especially favourable. The good promotion chances of the minority of men are attained at the expense of the majority of women. Lastly, in discussing changes over time, one has to make sure that the benchmarks remain the same. The difficulty with clerking is that the content of the job may have changed, so that people working as clerks all their lives may in fact be downwardly mobile in terms of the work that they actually do. More pertinently, the categories into which clerks may be promoted may also have changed. It may possibly be the case that clerks apparently promoted will continue to do the same work as before (see Crompton and Jones, 1981, for confirmation of this view). In order to assess this aspect of the market situation of clerks, therefore, one needs to know much more about the nature of clerical work.

The greatest change in the clerk's circumstances has occurred in the work situation and in the kind of work that clerks do (although for a review of the proletarianising situation of the nineteenth century clerk see Anderson, 1976, 1977; Crossick, 1977a). Furthermore, as we have already argued, market situation and work situation are closely linked, and part of the explanation of the declining market situation of the clerk lies in the rationalisation and mechanisation of the office. We have already discussed various accounts of these issues in Chapter 3 and we now try to take a more positive view of that evidence and argument.

Lockwood gives four reasons for supposing that the rationalising tendencies of modern office administration have not destroyed the personal and particular relationships of clerical work. First, the size of administrative unit is still smaller than that typical for manual employments. Secondly, the division of labour in the office tends to separate clerks from each other and places them in close proximity to management. Thirdly, clerical skills and qualifications have not been standardised. Fourthly, mechanisation has not extensively rationalised the work situation, because its application 'has so far been narrowly limited by the size of the administrative unit and the nature of clerical work itself' (1958, p. 96). However, we would suggest that Lockwood does not interpret some of his own arguments correctly and, much more significantly, the pace of change in office work has been greater than anyone might have expected. There is a continuing process affecting clerical work, which might roughly be described as proletarianisation, although the term is not without its dangers. This process, which moves at different speeds at different times and in different sectors of employment, has a number of closely connected features.

As Lockwood indicates, clerical work is characterised by a division of labour and this feature is becoming more pronounced. Not only is it possible to make productivity gains by splitting up the labour process into more and more steps, it is also possible to apply the 'Babbage Principle' and bring in less-skilled and lower-paid workers to perform work that has been made less demanding of skill by rationalising in this way. Splitting up the labour process makes each task more specialised. In the insurance industry, for example, the issuing of a policy, previously handled by a single underwriter, is now handled by several clerks each working to a closely specified set of routines (Crompton, 1979; De Kadt, 1979). An index of subdivision is provided by Glenn and Feldberg (1979), who point out that one large insurance company has 350 job titles for its 2,000 employees. As units of administration become larger (and they have), specialisation and subdivision make it possible to concentrate activities in pools in separate places. While this may at one time have been only true of typing, it now begins to extend to many facets of office work. Furthermore, with the introduction of increasingly expensive equipment such as word-processors, it actually becomes necessary to concentrate similar activities in order to make economic use of the machines. A familiar consequence of fragmentation of the labour process is the greater control that accrues to the management because each worker has control over a smaller part of the whole process. This suggests a curious feature of Lockwood's argument, for he seems to contend that the work situation of the clerk is greatly different from that of the manual worker precisely because of a greater division of labour and the resulting proximity of worker and manager. However, the point of fragmentation of the labour process is that it permits greater control of the process, whether the work is manual or non-manual. Again, the fact that clerk and immediate boss are thrown together on personal terms would suggest a greater degree of effective managerial control, although, ironically, fragmentation will undermine these personal relationships.

The rationalisation that permits greater management control also reduces the autonomy permitted to workers. The smaller the task performed, the greater the loss of independence. The typist operating an electric typewriter can set her work out in her own way and can, to some extent, pace herself. A word-processor, however, does not allow such a range of activities. The reorganisation and rationalisation of office work and the reduction of employee autonomy with the growth of managerial control are also all related to the increasing mechanisation of clerical work. As we indicated in Chapter 3, machines have been introduced into almost all areas. The pace of work is increasingly dictated by the machine which also demands very accurate input, particularly where computers are concerned. Deskilled white-collar workers become like workers on a production line. A typist working to telephone dictation, for example, will move on to the next piece of work as soon as she has finished her current one, since the equipment can store dictations.

As a result of rationalisation and mechanisation, clerks no longer use skills that may have been acquired to get the job in the first place; they are deskilled. Secretarial skills are given up in favour of routine, mechanical operations (CSE Microelectronics Group, 1980). As insurance policy writing becomes standardised, and hence suitable for computer operation, clerks trained in the mysteries of issuing appropriate policies at the correct premiums become mere adjuncts of the machine.

It would be a commonplace to say that most deskilled white-collar workers are employed in bureaucracies and always have been. However, in the sense that the activities of employees are being made more detailed, they are also more governed by rules; they are more bureaucratised. Each position in a more specialised division of labour has an implicit, and often explicit, rulebook attached to it, which incidentally permits the ready substitution of employees since no training is required beyond conformity to the rules. Indeed, bureaucratisation in the form of a network of rules is an absolute necessity for managements faced with the difficulties of reintegrating a labour process which has been fragmented in the interests of control, economy and productivity. Rules of conduct provide one means for ensuring that one step leads to another. All the processes that we have described have the final consequence of further separating conception from execution. With the rationalisation of the labour process, the fragmentation and standardisation of tasks, and the increasing bureaucratisation of administration, the mental labour content of white-collar jobs passes further up the hierarchy. The process of rationalisation has undermined the traditional sociological distinction between manual and non-manual work; clerks *are* manual workers (see Hill, 1981, ch. 9 for similar conclusions).

We conclude that it is fair to refer to the market and work situation of deskilled white-collar workers as proletarianised; the class places of these workers are subject to forces similar to those of the working class. However, one should be wary of using the concept, and the term, proletarianisation too freely. First, we join with Crompton (1980) in stressing proletarianisation as a process. It will not do simply to compare middle-class and working-class places at one particular time. Secondly, it is mistaken to compare the middle class with a working class which is considered as essentially an unfragmented proletariat simply waiting to have its true interests realised. Thirdly, we must distinguish a proletarianisation of condition from a proletarianisation of action. As we shall show in the next chapter, the latter does not directly follow from the former.

THE MARKET AND WORK SITUATION OF MIDDLE-CLASS PLACES: THE SERVICE CLASS

So far we have argued that the market and work situation of deskilled white-collar workers places them within the working class. We turn now to an account of the market and work situation of the 'upper' section of what is commonly called the middle class. We shall refer to this, for reasons that will soon become clear, as the service class.

In considering the market situation of the service class at various points (see Chapter 3 above and earlier discussion in this chapter, especially Table 7.1) our conclusion is that there is a substantial divergence of pay and various fringe benefits between the service class and deskilled white-collar workers. Another important point of difference in the market situation of these two groups lies in the notion of career.

One of the most significant features of the position of the service class is that most of the places of the class are located in bureaucracies. Bureaucracies function essentially as internal labour markets. In bureaucratic organisations most employees have a set of stable expectations about opportunities that will be open to them given their current performance in the job. They expect career rewards, having fulfilled specific and known requirements. This means that career lines in an organisation are well known. People know at what age they can expect to be where, and what risks and benefits attach to each point in the ladder (see Clements, 1958; Sofer, 1970). To be employed in a bureaucracy at a certain level implies the possession of expectations of increasing income, control and responsibility. For example, as Edwards (1979) shows, 'Polaroid, like other bureaucratically controlled firms, establishes promotion ladders and an internal market' (p. 182). New workers are recruited only for jobs on the bottom rungs which function as entry points to the bureaucracy. Bureaucratic careers, as stable sets of expectations, may seem not unlike those kinds of career available to manual workers who may move jobs within the same enterprise or within the same internal labour market, seeking improved earnings or easier work. However, such movement for workers usually involves trading off one benefit against another – wages against greater control, for example. The point about service-class careers is that employees gain advantages in all spheres as they progress up the bureaucratic ladder.

Service-class places are, therefore, places within bureaucracies and are likely to become increasingly so. As Goldthorpe says, 'Certainly, in present-day Britain, the centrality of the experience of career – often intra-occupational – mobility is entirely intelligible among members of the service class, whose working lives will have been largely shaped by bureaucratic, and typically *expanding* bureaucratic structures' (p. 227; author's emphasis). For Goldthorpe, it is the expansion of bureaucratic service-class places that is critical in understanding the pattern of social mobility in Britain since the war. In a sense, of course, deskilled white-collar workers also occupy places in a bureaucracy. However, like Dahrendorf (1959), we see these places as being subject to bureaucratic authority, while service-class places rather participate in the exercise of authority. Dahrendorf, it will be remembered, distinguishes positions which are on a bureaucratic ladder from those which are not. He also suggests that true bureaucrats, those participating in authority, are not identical with the ruling class since their authority is 'borrowed' from positions of more general authority outside the hierarchy. Bureaucracies therefore function as instruments, as Weber pointed out, and this provides the justification for Dahrendorf's use of the term 'service' class.

Careers within bureaucracies do not, therefore, only involve steadily improving pay and conditions. They also imply changes in the work situation. As we have already indicated, bureaucratic roles are positions of authority and control. Bureaucrats have to devise systems for the execution of tasks, have to divide them up into sub-tasks, and have to supervise and combine them. They have to impose order. Secondly, service class places also involve a relative freedom from control, providing a sphere of autonomy within which it is possible to organise and pace work as one likes, taking responsibility for the work done. Within limits, these places are self-defined. As Sofer (1970) indicates, this relative control over the working environment also means that the service-class workers can extend themselves if they wish, an opportunity denied to the clerk. Furthermore, this relative autonomy does not only apply to bureaucrats, but also to those technical specialists whose position Dahrendorf finds it so difficult to define. As Hales (1980) says of his work as a systems analyst: 'At the most basic level of the apparatus of work – time economy – my activity is more or less self-structured. This derives partly from managerial recognition that "problem-solving" is an open-ended process, and partly from the status of a "responsible" employee who is not expected to need close supervision' (p. 35). A third feature of the work situation of service-class places is that they typically involve mental labour, specifically the conception and design of labour processes. Design of this kind is, of course, not just a technical or conceptual matter, for labour-processes are not only defined by their technical place. As labour processes are designed to make a profit, they have also to be conceived in terms of control. In that service-class workers are conceptual workers, they also reinforce the system of control which they operate (see Chapter 6). The differences in work situation between the service class and deskilled white-collar work apparent from more abstract discussion are also revealed in anecdotal accounts of people's work lives. The description of the day-to-day work of the clerk in Fraser (1968, 1969), for example, contrasts vividly with the relative autonomy of the town planner or doctor. There is also no shortage of literary illustrations of the same theme. Orwell's insurance salesman in *Coming up for Air* (1939), for example, is an embodiment of failure, frustrated hopes and impossible fantasies. He is trapped in his routine, meaningless job which, from the point of view of the freedom it offers, he contrasts unfavourably with those of the working class. Similarly, Wells's shop-assistant, Kipps (1905), has an entirely routine existence in which he is closely controlled, a solution to which is only found when he eventually becomes a shop-keeper himself.

The work and market situation of the service class is also defined and reinforced by professional commitments. Many bureaucrats and specialists are members of the old-established professions and, to some extent, managerial occupations themselves are becoming professionalised. The effect of professional membership is to delimit spheres of competence within which a trained person can operate. Professions claim access to an esoteric body of knowledge and that only persons trained within the profession are competent in this area. Professionals, therefore, can be given autonomy and responsibility because they are, by definition, competent. At the same time, they must be given autonomy because only they are competent. Furthermore, the more a service-class place really does involve a technical expertise, the more its work and market situation will be defined by a profession. To a considerable extent, what control there is of service-class places is deputed to the professional associations. This control operates at two levels. First, access to many service-class places is regulated, and confined only to those who have been through the required period of training. Secondly, policing of those who have attained professional places is carried out according to the associations' codes of ethics.

Bureaucracy is, however, Janus-faced, for it is a system of constraint. Service-class workers benefit from bureaucratic employment in that they have relative autonomy, but they are also relatively constrained by bureaucratic rules and the aims of the organisation, whether they be the pursuit of profit, adequate medical care, or administration of government expenditure. The service class, it must be remembered, serves. There is therefore a potential conflict between professionalisation and bureaucratisation in respect of the work situation of the service class. The former strengthens service-class autonomy while the latter undermines it. A number of studies document this potential conflict (see, for example, Harries-Jenkins, 1970; Sofer, 1970). There are also disagreements as to the likely outcome of the conflict. Friedson (1973), for example, argues that professional authority will come to replace bureaucratic authority as knowledge becomes increasingly important for the discharge of work tasks. Oppenheimer (1973), on the other hand, suggests that bureaucratisation will erode the assertions of professional competence.

Both these accounts may well be right and they again direct attention to bureaucratisation and rationalisation as processes which continually affect the structure of work tasks. Thus rationalisation, which transforms the class situation of routine white-collar workers so thoroughly, also affects the lower reaches of the service class; it does not respect class boundaries. This process has the effect, however, of transferring autonomy, control and decision-making up the hierarchy, restricting the opportunities of those below. Rationalisation, therefore, does not affect all service-class places. A number of studies document the effect of rationalising tendencies on different occupations. Kraft (1979), for example, describes how computer programming, which originally included the whole process of software preparation, has become subdivided and rationalised (also see the discussion in Chapter 4, pp. 57–8). First, by fragmenting the labour process, three new occupations are created, systems analysts, programmers and coders, permitting a great reduction in the overall level of skill employed. Secondly, the breaking-up of the programme writing further into stages, so that less skilled but more specialised persons can work on particular kinds of sub-routines, further refines the labour process. Lastly, the use of canned programmes, higher-level languages and even programming by machine make further savings in labour cost. The effect of these processes is to create a class of programming managers who design a labour process for less skilled programmers. Leggatt (1970) points to the manner in which the work situation of teachers is degraded by employment in bureaucratic institutions. Larkin (1947) gives a literary illustration of the routine quality of librarian's work. Freeman (in Fraser 1968, 1969) shows how journalistic work is subdivided, with each journalist producing a small proportion of a whole story. In a more general way, Crompton and Jones (1981) present preliminary evidence which suggests that the content of some junior managerial work has become more 'proletarian' over time. Many middle- to lower-level managers spend very little of their time exercising what are commonly thought of as managerial functions. Indeed, the content of their job may differ little from that of their alleged subordinates. 'Manager', in this light, merely represents an empty job title.

STRUCTURE AND FUNCTION IN THE SERVICE CLASS

We have defined the service class in terms of market and work situation and have avoided a directly functional definition like that offered by many Marxist writers. Poulantzas, for example, conceives of the middle class as performing unproductive labour, while Carchedi argues that many white-collar workers are effectively performing capital functions. This, however, does not mean to say that a functional analysis is irrelevant to an account of the class position of the service class. On the contrary, it is crucial, for it is only by understanding what the service class does, what functions are performed within these places, that one can show how service-class places are generated and distributed within a capitalist economy. We argue that the service class performs the functions of control, reproduction and conceptualisation – necessary functions for capital in relationship to labour. Briefly, there are two crucial aspects of labour-power. On the one hand, unlike any other commodity, it cannot be produced by capitalists for profit. It is produced, or more accurately reproduced, outside capitalist relations within both civil society and the state (see Urry, 1981b). On the other hand, once the commodity labour-power, has been bought by the capitalist, it must then be reunited with the means of production. The direct labourer enters into a normal, active relationship with the means of production, a relationship determined by the nature and purpose of the particular work in question. Capitalist production necessarily involves the management of that labour-power in order that commodities produced can be separated from the direct producers. These two essential features of labour-power thus give rise to two functional requirements within any society in which capitalist relations are to be secured: first, that labour-power be 'reproduced', and secondly, that it be effectively 'controlled'. Labour processes also have to be conceived, and to the extent to which there is a clear separation of mental and manual labour and an increasing separation of the activities of conception and execution, the service class performs the function of conceptualisation. Changes in capitalism will affect the supply of places filling these three functions, of control, reproduction and conceptualisation. The increasing dominance of the socialisation of unproductive labour, for example, carries with it the requirement to conceive and control unproductive labour processes. However, an increase in the functional requirements and an increase in service-class places are not automatically produced by developments within the capitalist mode of production. They are also the product of struggles within and between classes.

Our argument so far has certain implications, particularly for the relations between the service class and other classes, which we shall now discuss.

The term 'service class' is apt, because, following Renner, it suggests that the class performs functions 'delegated' from capitalists. However, in one important respect we cannot agree with Renner, for, we suggest, capital has developed in such a manner as to affect the way that the capitalist class is constituted. Weber and many of his contemporaries signalled these changes by discussing the way in which individual capitalists are being replaced by a staff of functionaries. There is now widespread argument that the pattern of ownership of capitalist enterprises has changed considerably over the last century. It is less and less the case that firms are wholly or largely owned by individuals or families; they are increasingly owned, potentially at least, by very many people through the institution of share-ownership. Modern capitalism is therefore becoming 'depersonalised' both from the viewpoint of wealthy families whose property interests are now spread widely across more than one enterprise (see Scott, 1979, who notes the cross-national variations). Of course, ownership is being reconcentrated as financial institutions, pension funds, insurance companies and banks come to hold a larger proportion of company shares. However, this does not represent any return to personal ownership, since these institutions are similarly owned impersonally or are managed by boards of trustees. We should stress that this process of depersonalisation is not irreversible; it is not built into the logic of capitalism. Nor is it uniform across countries, as Scott (1979) clearly shows. Furthermore, it is an ongoing process which has certainly not been completed. We should also make it clear that we are not arguing that the nature of capitalism has been fundamentally altered by the changes in ownership. Institutional ownership often gives a wide measure of control and, as we have argued elsewhere in this chapter, control in an institutionally owned firm may mean much the same as in a personally owned firm. The spreading of ownership has also produced a fair degree of mutual ownership between financial and industrial or commercial institutions. Even pension funds, often celebrated as people's capitalism, are essentially financial institutions and especially where external fund managers are used they are inserted into a profit-making structure. As Minns (1980) says of the results of pension fund investment, 'financial institutions have gained additional levers to use in the pursuit of their main profit-making objectives' (p. 147).

However, although forms of control and the relationship between ownership and control have not greatly changed, the depersonalisation of ownership does have consequences for the constitution, and even existence, of the capitalist class. Of course, the reorganisation of property interests has not necessarily made propertied persons less wealthy; capitalist societies are still highly inegalitarian. Income, we have argued earlier, does constitute part of market situation, but it does not make up all of class position. That is largely dependent on work situation and the work situation of a capitalist class is crucially dependent on the personal ownership of the means of production. As there is an increasing separation of possession, economic ownership and legal ownership (Poulantzas, 1975) the work situation of capitalist class places is becoming increasingly less distinguishable from that of the service class. It makes less and less sense, therefore, to refer to the service class as a class 'in the middle'. Clearly, these changes in market and work situations are related to the discharge of capitalist functions of reproduction, control and conceptualisation. As these functions become increasingly delegated to a service class, specifically capitalist places are generated to a lesser extent (but for a contrast between 'personal' capitalists and bureaucrats see Fidler, 1981). It is emphatically not the case that there are no longer any capitalist functions, as some writers have argued. The deeper changes in capitalist society have not altered the requirements for these functions, but they have changed the manner in which the functions are organised into class places. In sum, the members of the service class are increasingly functionaries for capital, not for capitalists; services are not to any great extent performed for a distinct capitalist class.

There are, of course, still places with capitalist work situations, that is, personal ownership combined with control (possession and economic ownership). There is clearly great variability within the small capital sector, from small shop-keepers to fairly large industrial or financial enterprises, although there are relatively few really large firms still in private – personal or family – ownership in the UK (see Scott, 1979). Despite this variability, however, one of the features of their market and work situations that they have in common, besides personal ownership, is the fact that they are employers of labour-power. It would be mistaken to interpret the small capitalist sector as necessarily and irreversibly declining in its relationship with big capital. Thus, even if big capital is the dominant partner in this relationship, small capital is important as suppliers, customers, technologically advanced subcontractors or providers of productive services, as Gershuny (1978) shows. It is this close functional relationship between capitals that determines the relationship between the small capitalist class and the service class. The two classes both perform capital functions but the different nature of their places, defined by market and work situations, marks them off. They are therefore classes 'side-by-side' rather than hierarchically arranged one on top of the other.

It is important to note that the boundaries of classes naturally contain marginal class places as the various processes that we have identified continually affect the boundary positions. For example, we have noted how capitalist places are being converted into service-class places and also how lower management and professions are becoming relatively deskilled. Similarly, small capitalist places are marginal to the working class in the sense that they may lose the capacity of employing labour-power. Again, independent professional places exist at the margins of the service class and the small capitalist class. The creation of marginal places on the boundaries of classes is reflected in the mobility of persons across boundaries. Notoriously, self-employed workers slip in and out of the position of capitalist employer as their economic situation changes.

One further implication of our discussion so far is that there is an important difference between structure and function in the analysis of class (see Wright, 1978). There is a sense in which the structural and functional position of the service class coincide. That is, their market and work situation coincides with their functions of control, reproduction and conception. This is not true, however, of deskilled white-collar workers. We have argued that, structurally, the market and work situation of these workers places them within the working class. Functionally, however, they are unproductive workers partially involved in the control, reproduction and conceptualisation of labour processes. It may well be that the functional aspects of the position of deskilled white-collar workers become less critical as the important aspects of these functions become concentrated in the service class. However, the residual functional separation between deskilled white-collar workers and manual workers reinforces the differentiation within the working class which makes the notion of proletarianisation difficult to apply in any straightforward way. A final irony should be noted here. A structural, market and work, 'Weberian' definition may well put deskilled white-collar workers into the working class. A 'Marxist' functional definition, on the other hand, must argue against any such proletarianisation theory.

In this chapter we have argued that 'service class' is an apt term. Three of the writers discussed in Chapter 3 who have used the concept in apparently very different ways have, in our view, each identified one important feature of the class. Renner argues that the service class performs functions delegated from capital, Dahrendorf emphasises the importance of bureaucratic employment, while Goldthorpe assumes that the service class is at the top of a hierarchy of class positions. Further, we have suggested that the service class is best seen as produced by a hierarchy of processes. The mechanisms of the capitalist mode of production require the functions of conceptualisation, control and reproduction to be performed and they produce sets of places comprising specific market and work situations, which we call classes. In the case of the service class, there is a coincidence of function and class place, though not for deskilled white-collar workers. Persons with certain market capacities are recruited to class places. It should be noted that this view does not represent a simple choice of either Marxist or Weberian theory. Even if classes are defined by reference to market and work situations, one can only understand the generation of those situations by analysis of the workings of the capitalist mode of production and a specification of functions performed, especially in the stage of development in which unproductive labour is socialised. Furthermore, our discussion of market and work situations shows them to be closely interconnected. Work situation partially determines market situation, which is only partially autonomous, while market situation does not determine work situation.

In one very important respect it is misleading to refer to the way that class places are generated as if the relations between the various elements were necessary. In fact the relations are variable and depend heavily on class and other social struggles. Thus, the exact constitution of market and work situations is variable as is the number of places in each class. Struggles have a different effect on market and work situations, influencing the former more than the latter. As a corollary, the degree of class differentiation, expressed by differences in market and work situation, will also vary as the outcome of relations between and within existing classes. Again the way that persons are recruited to places is a function of processes which clearly differ from society to society. Since recruitment to the service class is largely based on the possession of credentials, the degree to which an education system is open to persons of all classes will determine the pattern of entry to the service class. Indeed, the manner in which persons are recruited to class is of crucial importance, not in directly determining class places, but in determining class and other social practices, which in turn influence those factors which determine class places.

We have argued in this chapter that, although classes are defined in terms of places with distinctive market and work situations, it is only possible to understand them by showing what the functional role of class places is. In turn, an interpretation of changes in these functions, and the way in which they are distributed into class places, is only achieved by an account of developments within the capitalist mode of production. We have also argued that one cannot account for the class structure of contemporary capitalist society as if it were uniquely determined by the economy, for the struggles of classes and other social forces affect the very processes that determine classes. This problem is discussed in Chapter 8.

8

Causal Powers, Struggles and Politics

In this chapter we shall consider some important dimensions of conflict and struggle which bear upon both the service class and deskilled white-collar workers. In the first section we shall analyse some general issues in the consideration of class struggles which are raised by Przeworski. We will make some general comments on the causal powers of different classes and on the conditions under which they may be realised. In the next section we shall consider two such determinants in more detail, namely, the constraints of organisation and some effects of the structuration of civil society. Finally, we shall analyse both the diverse forms of 'middle-class' struggle and the variety of consequences that they have, especially on the struggles of labour. Particular attention will be paid to the professions and the elaboration of the division between mental and manual knowledge.

PROBLEMS IN THE ANALYSIS OF SOCIAL STRUGGLES

Przeworski's central claim is twofold: first, that economic, political and ideological conditions together structure the realm of struggles and these have, as their effect, the organisation, reorganisation, or disorganisation of social classes; and secondly, that the effects of these struggles in turn transform those very conditions under which such classes are formed (see 1977). Thus classes are formed as the result of struggles, these struggles in turn affect the very conditions which structure such struggles, and the effects on classes are in part indeterminate since they depend upon the dynamic interrelations between classes.

Przeworski argues that these claims entail a systematic breaking with the basic problematic of Marx's analysis of social class. In this problematic the class-in-itself is defined at the level of the 'base' – which is simultaneously objective and economic. Class-for-itself is that class characterised by organisation, solidarity and consciousness. The main issue under this approach is to identify the conditions that lead the former to develop into the latter. Przeworski maintains that there have been two characteristic positions: the deterministic, in which objective relations are necessarily transformed into subjective relations; and the voluntaristic, in which classes are only viewed as being formed through the intervention of the external agent, the party. As an example of a text caught in the trap of this problematic, Przeworski considers two particular problems in Kautsky's *The Class Struggle* (1971). The first is that Kautsky seems to have believed that by 1890 or so the proletariat had already been formed into a class – and would forever remain as a class fulfilling its historic mission, albeit aided and abetted by the party. In other words, there was a once-and-for-all transformation of the class-in-itself into the class-for-itself; once transformed it was then merely a question of time before the proletariat realised its purpose or telos. A second problem, which is related to this, is that Kautsky presumed that the meaning of the term 'proletariat' was unambiguous. However, by the end of the century this was not the case; by no means all those workers who were separated from the means of production were productive manual labourers. Just what was the likely class allegiance of non-productive salaried employees, who were none the less wage-labourers? Kautsky treats them inadequately, failing to explain the development of the so-called new middle class. Indeed, Kautsky in the main suggests that people only engage in the tasks of office worker, middleman, and so on, because they cannot find productive employment elsewhere and they are separated from the means of production. In order to survive they are forced to resort to the superfluous pursuits of 'middlemen, saloonkeepers, agents, intermediaries etc.' (Kautsky, 1971, p. 85).

Przeworski does not, of course, suggest that all Marxists have treated the problem of the new middle class so inadequately (see Chapters 4 and 5 above for discussion of the most interesting contributions). But he does maintain that the issue of the new middle class raises particular difficulties for the class-in-and-for-itself problematic (see Stark, 1980, for a related critique). He argues that it is impossible to specify particular structural determinations which will unambiguously and uniquely account for the distinctive political positions which are taken up. Indeed, these structural determinations are not to be properly viewed as objective and outside the class struggles which they are supposedly meant to explain. And furthermore, much struggle is not simply between already constituted classes – it is to establish a class. It is a struggle about class before it is a struggle between classes (see Przeworski, 1977, pp. 371–3). One important consequence is that class organisations may well be temporarily discontinuous.

Przeworski also maintains that at least half the adult population in the USA is to be seen as relatively surplus labour, and the form that this labour takes is not directly structured by capitalist relations and forces of production. Capitalist social relations do not distribute this surplus labour into specific places-to-be-occupied. Surplus labour may take the form of partially underemployed labour within the state, of a reserve army to regulate wage levels, of a generally shorter working week, and so on. Which of these is found in any conjuncture depends on forms of class struggle, not upon the inherent functioning of the capitalist economy.

We will briefly mention some difficulties encountered in Przeworski's analysis, although some of his arguments, as we shall see, are of particular importance. First, he provides little in the way of illustration of exactly how struggles do change structures, or how the reproduction of certain structures does depend upon particular forms of struggle. Przeworski does not investigate how this may involve a highly complex, paradoxical process in which the 'structure' may be such that it will produce forms of struggle which, although consistently unsuccessful, nevertheless ensure as their necessary effect the reproduction of the structure (for example, of wage-labourers and the struggle for socialism).

Secondly, Przeworski confuses two distinctions. On the one hand, there is that between the structural determination of a class, and the later, potential, emergence of that class as a socio-political force engaging in struggle. And, on the other, there is that between the theory of the determining structures, and the concrete forms of socio-political struggle in which that class engages. Thus, on the first distinction, it is perfectly proper to criticise certain theorists for ignoring the way in which classes as socio-political forces affect the structures which in part helped to generate such social forces. Yet, on the later distinction, this is invalid since the concrete forms of struggle cannot affect the theory of such structures, except in an indirect sense. Yet, even on the first distinction, it is curious to characterise such class struggles as necessarily non-structural, since this would seem to reproduce something of the classical determinism/voluntarism dichotomy. And further, it presumes that all structures are equivalent, that the economic, political and ideological structures are homologous.

Finally, there are some difficulties entailed by the notion of class struggle employed by Przeworski, among many others. To designate a particular struggle as a class struggle may entail one or more of three claims:

(1) that the overwhelming majority of the participants mobilised are members of the class in question and that many members of that class support that struggle – we will call this the membership-criterion;

(2) that the content of the struggle reflects either or both the short and long-term interests of the class in question – the interests-criterion;

(3) that the conflict is in some sense generated by the underlying struggle between the classes – the causal-criterion.

Przeworski does not make clear which of these senses of class struggle he is employing. Nor does he acknowledge that the identification of the consequences of 'struggle' is highly problematic. This is partly because of the difficulty of establishing the connections between specific day-to-day forms of struggle, on the one hand (strikes, lock-outs, demonstrations, working-to-rule, etc.), and longer-term social processes, on the other. But also it is exceptionally difficult to establish relevant counterfactuals; just what would have happened in the absence of this particular struggle, or the struggle of this class? The processes are necessarily ongoing and dynamic and it is difficult to demonstrate the effect of one particular social element within the whole.

We mentioned earlier that Przeworski mistakenly presumes that all the structures within capitalist societies (the economic, political and the ideological) exhibit a homologous form. This raises a more general issue – namely, just what kinds of things are social structures, what constitutes their character and how do they generate empirical events? And in particular, what are classes? Are they mere sets of empirical events or are they things possessing causal powers that are to some degree analogous to those of, say, a mode of production (see Keat and Urry, 1982, 'Postscript')? We believe that classes are to be viewed as entities possessing causal powers, powers in other words to generate empirically observable occurrences, and therefore we reject the notion that social reality is to be viewed as sets of discrete events. Rather this event-ontology should be replaced by an ontology of relatively enduring entities, and their interrelationships, which have the power to produce empirical events (see Harré and Madden, 1975, on these different ontologies).

This view can be counterposed to two particularly problematic positions within the Marxist tradition. In the first, classes are seen as reducible to the objective determinants which generate them. Class practices merely result from, or are released by, these determinants. On this view, identifiable in parts of Poulantzas (see 1975, 'Introduction'), classes and their struggles do not possess causal powers. It is the objective structures that possess such powers; the view that classes may have them as well is viewed as a historicist deviation. In the second and opposing position, it is held that the capitalist and proletarian classes each possess a distinct essence and that, as history proceeds, these essences will emerge. In the case of the proletariat its essence is to destroy capitalist relations and ultimately to replace it with a communist alternative, that is, to redeem the whole of humanity through the necessary realisation of its own essence. On this view the entities which possess causal powers within capitalism are the two major classes, the capitalist and the proletariat.

Both views are problematic. We have already seen some objections to the former in Przeworski. The latter view raises three particular difficulties. First, it ignores the other entities within capitalist societies which also possess causal powers: the relations of production, the state, civil society, other classes, and so on. Secondly, it may be presumed that the proletariat in particular possesses only one set of powers, namely, to revolutionise capitalist relations and realise true communism. But while in the natural sciences, it does seem reasonable to presume that things do possess only one set of powers, for example, that of dynamite to explode, in the social world this is not the case. Indeed, it can be plausibly argued that Marx himself shows elsewhere that the proletariat possesses alternative causal powers, to 'reform' capitalist societies, and that this set of powers may well be realised instead (see C. Johnson, 1980; also McCarthy, 1978). And finally, in this essentialist view, it may be presumed that nothing will happen to frustrate the realisation of the supposed powers. Yet since the social world is in fact comprised of irreducibly interconnected entities, then these entities provide the very conditions for each of them realising their particular powers. It is highly likely that the other entities will be combined in such a way that the causal powers of any given class are not fully realised (see further discussion in Keat and Urry, 1982, 'Postscript', and in Urry, 1981b, ch. 5, on how the causal powers of civil society will frustrate the causal powers of the proletariat).

What, then, are the causal powers of the service class? They are to restructure capitalist societies so as to maximise the divorce between conception and execution and to ensure the elaboration of highly differentiated and specific structures within which knowledge and science can be maximally developed. They are thus to deskill productive labourers and to maximise the educational requirements of places within the social division of labour. This implies the minimising of non-educational/non-achievement criteria for recruitment to such places; and the maximising of the income and resources devoted to education and science, and more generally to the sphere of 'reproduction'. The middle classes will thus possess powers to enlarge the state structures by which they can organise and 'service' private capitalist enterprises. Our argument here is briefly that certain changes in contemporary capitalism have considerably increased the degree to which the causal powers of the service class have been realised. This has resulted from certain processes by which both capital and labour have weakened powers within contemporary capitalism. We have already noted the 'depersonalisation' of capital which is connected to its internationalisation. As a consequence there are important elements of each individual nation-state which are relatively undetermined by a specific capitalist class. Labour has been weakened because of the processes by which knowledge, skill and control have been separated off and embodied within distinct middle-class places. The increase in the complexity of contemporary forms of knowledge strengthens the causal powers of the middle classes, while weakening those of labour. Also the increased hypermobility of capital, that it can be readily moved from region to region or from nation to nation, regardless of the social or political costs, also weakens labour, which by contrast is relatively immobile having to accept the forms of employment offered by capital.

Thus, the causal powers of the service class are relatively strong in contemporary capitalism. There are a number of further points to make, though. First, there are important struggles between the service class and deskilled white-collar workers – struggles which have different effects within different sectors, depending in part on the form of knowledge involved (see the discussion above of Jamous and Peloille, p. 76) and its relationship to capital. Secondly, although we take classes to possess causal powers, it does not follow that aspects of a given society are direct expressions of those powers. Thus, for example, the state is not purely the instrument of the economically dominant class, nor are ideologies to be seen as simply class-structured and determined. Rather, the conjunctural features of a given society represent the form and degree to which the causal powers of the relevant entities are realised. And thirdly, the degree to which such powers of a class are realised depends upon, not only its mutually antagonistic relations with other classes, but also its constitutive forms of intra-class organisation and interconnectedness. In the next section we shall consider both issues in detail – namely, the likely organisation form taken by the middle classes in struggle, and the process by which the service class may be formed as a class out of the pertinent divisions of civil society. The realisation of causal powers by the middle classes depends upon establishing and sustaining a multiplicity of appropriate 'collectivities-in-struggle' – we shall consider some determinants of their formation. However, this investigation takes us well away from the traditional issue of the Boundary Problem – as Stark says (in an article which, like Przeworski, criticises the 'in-itself/for-itself' problematic):

> In attempting to defend their claims to technical expertise or to maintain the currency value of their certified degrees, the members of these new occupations stand not with one foot in the working class and one foot in the capitalist class but with one foot in a professional association and one foot in a bureaucratic (corporate or state) organization. The constellation of relations of conflict and alliance between these associations and other organizations arising from work, community, and political life must be the object of study in the analysis of class relations in the current period. (Stark, 1980, p. 119)

ORGANISATIONAL FORMS AND CIVIL SOCIETY

In this section we begin by considering an aspect neglected by most if not all the authors writing on these topics, that is, what kinds of organisational form the middle classes are able to develop. This requires some discussion of the analysis by Offe and Wiesenthal (1980) of the contrasting logics of collective action engaged in by labour and capital.

Offe and Wiesenthal argue that labour and capital show substantial differences with respect to the functioning and performance of their associations, and that these differences are both the consequence and the manifestation of the particular antagonistic class relations in which they are situated. The crucial feature of labour is its individuality; it is atomised and divided by competition. Moreover, labourers cannot merge, merely associate. Also, because of the indissoluble links between labourers and their labour-power, associations of labour must organise a wide spectrum of the needs of labour. Capital, by contrast, is united and is merely organised to maximise profits, this being a matter which can generally be left to decisions by technical experts. And at the same time, labour has to concern itself far more systematically with the well-being of capital than capital has to concern itself with the conditions of labour. Offe and Wiesenthal thus demonstrate that the associations of labour are defensive, they are responses to the collective organisation of capital. The latter also organise further in response to the associations of labour, in either informal co-operation or employers' associations, sometimes mediated by the state. Thus, capital possesses three forms of organisation: the firm itself, informal co-operation between firms and the employers' association; labour, by contrast, has merely one. It would appear never to be worthwhile for labour to engage in collective action – capital would always seem certain to win since there are far fewer individuals involved, they are more united and they possess clearer goals and greater resources. Thus Offe and Wiesenthal maintain that for the associations of labour to be viable an alternative form of organisation has to develop, which they term 'dialogical'. This involves, not merely aggregating the individual resources of the association members to meet the common interests of the membership, but also, and more distinctively, defining a collective identity. Labour (and, as we shall see, other subordinate social groupings) can only transform existing relationships by overcoming the relatively greater costs of engaging in collective action, as compared with capital. And this can only be achieved by deflating the standards by which such costs are assessed within their collectivity. The establishment of this collective identity is essential since it is the only means by which the subjective deflation of the costs of organisation can be effected. Moreover, it is only labour (or at least the relatively powerless) who may develop this non-utilitarian form of collective action, a form in which it is held that the costs of being a member of the organisation are not assessed instrumentally. The interests of labour thus can only be met through their redefinition in terms of collective identity (see Offe and Wiesenthal, 1980, p. 79). Capital, by contrast, can merely operate in terms of aggregating given interests. Their associations will be based on individualistic, instrumental forms of collective action which will have the effect of preserving their dominant position. This point relates to another crucial distinction. The organisations of labour rest upon the 'willingness to act', those of capital on the 'willingness to pay'. For the latter then there is no problem involved in maximising size; for the former this generates profound dilemmas. This is partly because an increase in size will probably produce a greater degree of bureaucratisation – and if this is so it will undermine that organisation's ability to mobilise its power to act. And it is also because an increase in size will increase the heterogeneity of members' occupations and interests, and hence will make it more difficult to establish the collective identity necessary for common action. Indeed, the larger the organisation, the more heterogeneous are the interests that have to be reconciled – not merely those of maximising members' wages, but also of ensuring security of employment, some control over the work process, and pleasant working and living conditions (see p. 82). Unlike organisations of capital, which can create and maintain the integration of its membership in a one-dimensional 'monological' manner, organisations of labour are involved in a complex and contradictory process of expressing/forming/sustaining a common identity – an identity which cannot be assessed in purely instrumental terms. The power of capital exists without organisation, the power of labour only exists with organisation, but it is an organisation which is precariously established. The organisation in part has to function 'dialogically' in that the activity and views of the membership have to be represented and embodied so as to sustain the necessary collective identity.

Thus far we have merely established some formal differences in organisation between capital and labour; Offe and Wiesenthal summarise these by arguing that while the organisations of capital are 'monological', those of labour have to be both 'monological' and 'dialogical'. However, they then turn to consider the pattern of interests articulated by such organisations; in particular, the relative degrees of interest-distortion between the different classes. Compared with labour, the interests of capital are far less ambiguous, controversial, or likely to be misperceived. This is, first, because this interest is generally accepted and supported, especially by the state and other key institutions. Secondly, the interest is 'monological' – capitalists do not have to consult in order to reach common understanding and agreement. The 'true' interest of labour, by contrast, can only be realised 'dialogically', through collectively going beyond given existing interests. Thirdly, the correction of interests will occur more quickly and directly for capital – errors will be directly visible and manifest, while labour may receive no such indications of error. Fourthly, since many of the dominant conceptions, theories, forms of representation, and so on, are in part 'capitalistic', it requires much greater communicative and organisational efforts on the part of labour to identify, develop and sustain its alternative interests. Hence, in order to achieve an equal accuracy in the awareness of its interests as compared with capital, labour has to expend vastly greater efforts (see Offe and Wiesenthal, 1980, pp. 91–2; Jacoby, 1978). Moreover, the greater institutionalisation of liberal political forms and modes of political theorising, then the greater the difficulties that are created for labour to overcome these distortions of interest. Liberalism, in other words, opposes those forms of 'dialogical' organisation which are, for Offe and Wiesenthal, essential for the realisation of the interests of labour. Liberalism thus favours the interests of capital because the latter are individualistic or 'monological'. Class conflict, then, is not just about the ends of politics, but is also a conflict about the forms, about what means are necessary in order to articulate the undistorted interests of subordinate classes (and, we might add, of other social groupings).

Offe and Wiesenthal further maintain that political struggle does not merely occur between labour and capital but is a conflict within labour itself, that is, over the forms of organisation, between the 'monological' and the 'dialogical'. They do briefly explore the imposition of individualistic political forms upon the organisations of labour, through, for example, limitations on areas of activity, the institutionalisation or juridification of alternative organisational forms, and so on (see Offe and Wiesenthal, 1980, pp. 99–103). But generally they consider that there are imperatives within labour itself which tend to generate 'monological' political forms, or what they characterise as 'opportunism'. By this they mean: (*a*) the inversion of the means/end relationship, with the institutionalisation of the former (the dialogical mode depends upon prioritising the latter); (*b*) the prioritising of immediate, short-term accomplishments; (*c*) the emphasis upon quantitative criteria for recruitment and mobilisation. What then generates opportunism, the shift from the 'dialogical' to the 'monological' mode of organisation?

They suggest a five-stage model for the development of labour organisations. Stage 1 is the formation of a collective identity, with a small size, strong willingness to act, low bureaucratisation and strongly 'dialogical'. Stage 2 is the possession of some power because it has threatened to act – yet it faces contradictory pressures. On the one hand, it must continue to appear a threat to capital – it must continue to recruit and mobilise; yet, on the other hand, it must not threaten its existence by continuously acting and hence reducing the gains to be achieved from threatening to act. Two resolutions are possible: either a reversion to stage 1, or a move to stage 3. Here the organisation's survival is made as independent as possible of the motivation, collective identity and willingness to act of the members in particular, by the substitution of external support and institutional recognition particularly by the state (often in social democratic parties). This is accompanied by maximising the independence of the organisation's functionaries from the membership, in other words, by displacing 'dialogical' relations through securing certain limited chances of success while escaping the threat to the organisation's survival. At stage 4 the external guarantees are withdrawn in whole or part because of changes in economic/political conditions. At stage 5, in response to 4, a fraction within the organisation restores collective action and challenges the opportunist strategy so far developed. Overall, Offe and Wiesenthal wish to show that this strategy is none the less a rational response to certain organisational imperatives, but that in general there are very good reasons why the monological will replace the dialogical as the predominant form of organisation.

How, though, does this argument relate to the analyses of the middle classes and the possible logics of collective action and forms of interest-distortion that they may demonstrate? First of all, there is a much greater chance of interest-distortion in the case of the 'middle classes' than in the case of capital and labour. This is because of their location 'between' the two main classes and hence of the difficulty of identifying their interests. In particular, it could only be through exceptionally well-developed dialogical processes that the middle classes could come to a relatively 'uncontaminated' realisation of their interests. However, not only are the middle classes more subject to interest-distortion than is the working class – but they are even less likely to develop a compensating 'dialogical' form of organisation. The main reason for this is that the middle-class organisations (especially white-collar unions) have developed at a later stage than the organisations of the working class, many or most of which have already reached stages 2 or 3 in Offe and Wiesenthal's scheme. This means that middle-class organisations operate in the context of organisations that are already organised 'opportunistically', that concentrate upon means rather than ends, that prioritise short-term gains and that employ quantitative criteria for recruitment and mobilisation. New organisations have to compete with these, and this means they will employ similar criteria for organisational success, namely, the achievement of a large and growing membership and short-term economic gains. This is thus the sense in which organisations of middle-class labour become 'proletarianised', that they operate under the same criteria of success and with a similar organisational form. It is also the case that many subjects occupying middle-class places will tend to reject a 'dialogical' organisational form, believing, falsely in large part, that this is synonymous with the organisation of labour *per se*. This means that, although certain organisations of labour may develop a dialogical form, stages 4 and 5, this is extremely unlikely in the case of middle-class labour.

This analysis of organisational form shows that the concept of the 'proletarianisation' of the middle classes is more problematic than was seen in Chapters 3 and 4 above. In particular: (*a*) the development of a socialist/proletarian interest is exceptionally difficult and, by contrast, only the capitalist class is likely to be able to develop a relatively undistorted identification of interests; (*b*) there are two modes of 'proletarian' organisation, the monological and the dialogical, but it is only the latter that is likely to ensure a relatively undistorted identification of interest; (*c*) the middle classes will develop only monological organisational forms, since the function of their organisations generally consists of mobilising as many individuals as possible (or who are qualified) for direct economic advantage (the importance of education and career serves to reinforce the individualism of the membership, and hence the monological form of the organisation; only in this sense then is there proletarianisation of action); (*d*) the increased importance of the middle classes means a further extension of monological organisations, and the reduced significance of the dialogical form: a concentration upon means rather than ends, on short-term gains, and on quantitative criteria of success (in the UK the left-wing, 'proletarian' ASTMS is the paradigm case); (*e*) to the extent to which non-monological forms develop, they are more likely among non-class groupings, especially of race and gender.

We shall now discuss this last point in greater detail, considering the constraints upon the struggles of deskilled white-collar workers and the service class resulting from certain forms of structuration within civil society and the state. It is often held that such determinants of struggle and conflict are less significant than the class conflict between capital and labour – and this is because the latter is a conflict common to all capitalist societies (see the discussion in Parkin, 1979, p. 32). These other sources of structuration are variable in their impact and are therefore, it is argued, less important. However, we disagree with this in relation to the middle classes precisely because of their constitution as 'classes-in-struggle'. In such a situation it is these other sources of structuration which may well be paramount – the realisation of the causal powers of the service class and of white-collar workers depends upon minimising the significance of these alternative forms of structuration. In other words, the characteristics of these persons recruited to these classes are crucial for identifying the possible realisation of their powers. We are not going to consider all such forms here, merely changes (1) in the sexual composition, (2) in the spatial distribution and (3) in state and informal employment.

(1)   It is now well known that there has been a great expansion in recent years in the numbers and proportion of women in paid employment, especially of married women and of women occupying middle-class places (see Routh, 1980). This has some important consequences.

(*a*)   If, as is increasingly common, both partners in a household are employed, then this will tend to reduce the mobility of labour since it will often be difficult to find alternative work for both in the area to which a move is being contemplated. One consequence of this, at least in periods of labour shortage, is that it causes capital to be increasingly concerned to identify 'pools' of available labour, which are, in many cases, female. Indeed, the availability of such pools of female labour may be important in the very structuring of places within the social division of labour.

(*b*)   Increasing numbers of households contain members who occupy places which cut across conventional class boundaries. In particular, many women are deskilled white-collar workers – while their male partners either are or have been 'working class' (see West, 1978, p. 233; Murgatroyd, 1981). Also, with unemployment/redundancy many males have drifted out of the formal economy, so constituting part of the 'excluded labour force'. These developments mean that it is incorrect to categorise households simply on the basis of the male's position within the formal economy (see West, 1978; Eichler, 1980, pp. 107–9).

(*c*)   This is reinforced by the considerable growth in upward mobility resulting from the socialisation of unproductive labour. For women this considerable upward mobility is overwhelmingly into the 'intermediate class' (see Heath, 1981), roughly what we term deskilled white-collar workers.

(*d*)   The division between the service class and deskilled white-collar workers is increasingly a division between males and females. Stewart *et al.* (1980) show that where there are males within the 'intermediate class' either they are young and generally on their way up into the service class, or they are older and have been mobile out of the working class. That the characteristic pattern of female mobility is only short run to become deskilled white-collar workers is a major basis for the generation of consequence *e*.

(*e*)   Feminist struggles are oriented around patriarchal relations. These are not just directed against male capitalists and state bureaucrats, but also against males within the working and service classes. It is possible that this illustrates Weber's thesis of periodic oscillation between class politics and status group politics (struggles over gender being an example of the latter; see Parkin, 1979, pp. 34–5, on ethnic struggles); it is more likely, though, that struggles around gender will be a relatively persistent characteristic of politics in contemporary capitalism. If so, it is a reflection of how the rapid socialisation, and especially the feminisation, of unproductive labour has further weakened conventional class politics. This is because of the generally lower unionisation and politicisation of women, the divisions between the sexes which they engender, and the way they move working class politics away from the centre of the political stage. Indeed, further struggles over the sex-typing of different occupations are a certain consequence of the continued desire of women to enter the labour market, combined with the reduced possibilities of employment for both men and women due to the rapidly shrinking formal economy (see Gershuny and Pahl, 1979, on the changing relations between the formal, household and informal economies; and Bell, 1979, on working-class demoralisation and the apparent need for new forms of moral identification and collective struggle with the development of post-industrial society).

(2)   There are important international variations in the development and effectiveness of different classes, such as the earlier and more extensive growth of middle classes in the USA compared with France; this occurred anyway in the context of an already strong labour movement (see p. 80 above on the PMC). However, we shall concentrate here on intranational variations. In particular, we can suggest that four of the local stratification structures now of contemporary relevance are as follows:

(*a*)   large national or multinationals as dominant employers – small service class – large number of deskilled white-collar workers – large working class and informal economy;

(b) state as dominant employer – large service class – large number of white-collar workers – declining working class – high employment of women;

(c) traditional small capitals as dominant employers – large petty bourgeois sector – small service class – small number of deskilled white-collar workers – large male working class – low level of female employment;

(d) private service sector capitals as dominant employers – largish service class and largish number of deskilled white-collar workers, both highly feminised – small working class. (See Urry, 1981a, for further discussion on this and the following argument.)

Two consequences follow from these very schematic suggestions. First, the impact of different classes will vary within these different localities, the service class being more effective in *b* and *d* rather than *a* and *c*. But secondly, such variations in local class structures will produce an increased sense of spatial deprivation and, as a consequence, the organisation of politics based upon the inferiority of one's own class structure *vis-à-vis* that of other areas. So even if there is no increase in conventional indicators of spatial inequality, deprivation *vis-à-vis* other regions may well grow (see Buck and Atkins, 1978; Buck, 1979). This may generate local social movements concerned with defending the local social structure against capital and the national state. Such 'local social movements' are an important consequence of new tendencies in the international division of labour (see Fröbel *et al.*, 1980), tendencies which weaken forms of class-structured politics (see Cooke, 1980).

(3) Three distinct fractions can be identified among the service class and deskilled white-collar workers: (*a*) the traditional petty bourgeoisie which comprises a separate and subordinated form of social labour which once was declining but which, because of the 'informal economy', may be increasingly important (see Gershuny and Pahl, 1979); (*b*) the middle-class state sector which in general does not directly control labour, or directly oppose capital; its politics are structured by the attempt both to expand state activities, and to oppose elements of hierarchical control (see Baudelot *et al.*, 1974, in particular; and Dunleavy, 1980, more generally); and (*c*) the middle-class private sector which *in toto* directly opposes capital, controls labour, and will tend to oppose extensions of the state. Hence, even economically, conflicts and struggles are not patterned in terms of one contradiction within a single mode of production. Various forms of struggle are possible since there are diverse 'main enemies' for these different fractions: for (*a*), the formal economy and the state; for (*b*), private capital and the controllers of the state apparatuses; and for (*c*), labour, capital *and* the state. Each may give rise to struggles, and

although these will increasingly take a labourist form, the struggle itself will involve systematic attempts to prevent the proletarianisation of such labour.

To conclude this section, we return to the analysis of organisational form and suggest that organisations will be less likely to be dialogical: (1) the more that already existing organisations are monological in form; (2) the greater the number and diversity of practices within civil society; (3) the more that a civil society is 'horizontally' rather than 'vertically' organised; (4) the earlier and larger the growth of the middle classes has been within that society.

Points (1) and (2) are fairly clear and have in part been discussed already. We shall now briefly consider (3) and (4). On the former, whether a civil society is horizontally organised refers to the degree to which its constitutive associations and organisations are independent of, and relatively unstructured by, the relations and forces of production, on the one hand, and the state, on the other. A horizontally organised civil society is found where there are a large number of social groupings and other social practices which are non-class-specific, and which give rise to relatively autonomous forms of representation within the state. By contrast the civil society is vertically organised when these organisations and associations are class-specific and there is little independent political representation. Very broadly speaking, as capitalism developed, there was an initial shift towards greater vertical organisation; while in the later stages there has been a tendency towards greater horizontal organisation. The latter shift has been associated with an exceptionally marked increase in the diversity of civil society in contemporary capitalism. But although many such organisations depend on their partial commodification, they do not simply reflect the divisions of interest generated within the economy. What is distinctive in contemporary capitalism is the enormous range of different classes and social groupings which struggle to improve their material circumstances – and they do so on bases which are diverse, which shift from issue to issue, which may conflict, and will be organised monologically. It is only where a civil society tends to vertical organisation, where the divisions in the economy are closely reflected throughout most of the organisations and associations of civil society, that dialogical forms will develop and be sustained.

We shall now consider point (4) above, namely, that the earlier and larger the growth of the middle classes within a particular capitalist society, the greater the likelihood that the organisations within civil society will be monological rather than dialogical. This is because the growth and development of large middle classes has the following effects: first, to increase the diversity of civil society, secondly, to reduce the vertical organisation and the degree to which organisations are class-dependent; thirdly, to ensure that their organisations will have had time to develop monologically, a process which can be seen even in many of the alternative

organisations generated in the last twenty years within Western capitalism. The groups apparently most able to resist the shift towards the
monological form are some of those that have developed within the
women's movement (see Rowbotham *et al.*, 1980).

In this section we have considered the determinants of the causal
powers of the middle classes. In the next we shall consider the degree to
which those powers have been realised.

SOCIAL STRUGGLES AND THEIR CONSEQUENCES

We can begin by noting that among those occupying service-class and
deskilled white-collar places there are a wide variety of political practices.
In contemporary Britain these range from: on the right, the Middle Class
Association, the National Viewers' and Listeners' Association, the
National Festival of Light, and other 'symbolic crusades', the National
Association for Freedom, various ratepayers' associations, patriotic
grouping, the National Front and the Association of Self-Employed
People; and on the left, environmentalist and amenity groups, CND, feminist groups, white-collar trade unionism, counter-cultural groupings,
far-left political parties and the Labour Party (see Parkin, 1968; Nugent
and King, 1977; King and Nugent, 1979; Garrard *et al.*, 1979). Partly this
diversity supports the arguments of Roberts *et al.* (1977) and King and
Nugent (1979), among others, that there is increasing fragmentation of
the contemporary middle class. It also suggests that there is little likelihood of independent unified political action by *the* 'middle class' on the
scale of the Mittelstand associations in pre-Nazi Germany or the Pouja-
distes in France (on the former, see Lebovićs, 1969; Blackbourn, 1977). It
is also the case that a great deal of 'middle class' politics is premised upon
the rejection of the notion either that there is a distinctive middle class, or
that there are distinctive middle classes. Indeed the 'Middle Class Association' floundered in part because of its apparent advocacy of class
politics, namely, protecting the interests of the middle class (see King and
Nugent, 1979, p. 3).

We shall now consider some of the consequence of such forms of
politics and more generally of strong middle classes; at this stage we shall
not distinguish between the effects of the service class and those of deskilled white-collar workers. Probably the most elaborate discussion of this
issue is to be found within the 'functionalist analysis' of the middle
classes. De Tocqueville, for example, argued that the growth of the
middle class undermines the clarity of a simply dichotomised society of
rich and poor – as a result the rich did not form an identifiable class whose
wealth could be easily plundered (see 1966, pp. 824–5; Urry, 1973a, pp.
57–8; as well as Aristotle, 1962, pp. 211–12). Lewis and Maude have
most amplified this view, arguing that the middle classes served a whole
range of economic and political functions especially in nineteenth-century

Britain (1949; and see Bradley, 1975; W. Weber, 1975; Hutber, 1977). These included the development of new sciences and other forms of knowledge, the increasing of national wealth, the development of notions of individual achievement and of the possibilities of upward mobility, and the stabilising of society through preventing its domination either by a single elite or by the state. Some of the economic functions of the middle classes have also been elaborated in the sociology of development. Emphasis has here been placed on the functional contribution either of an entrepreneurial middle class (see McClelland, 1961), or of a newly educated elite who would 'modernise' their society (see the critical discussion in Dore, 1976).

These 'functionalist' analyses are of course problematic, particularly in the fact that they ignore some very substantial dysfunctions. For example, the development of the professional middle class in nineteenth-century Britain, and its separation from the capitalist class, was in part also responsible for the decline of Victorian Britain and the low status attached to work in industry (see Reader, 1966, pp. 202–6; Perkin, 1969, pp. 437–54; Wiener, 1981). Matthew Arnold talked of:

> a middle class cut in two ... of a professional class brought up on the first plane, with fine and governing qualities, but without the idea of science: while that immense business class, which is becoming so important a power in all countries, on which the future so much depends ... is in England brought up on the second plane, but cut off from the aristocracy and professions, and without governing qualities. (Arnold, 1964, pp. 308–9)

See also Margaret Drabble's *The Ice Age* (1977), p. 22, for her professional middle-class hero's thoughts on a job in industry.

Likewise, the growth of secondary and higher education in Third World countries has been partly dysfunctional – not only in terms of cost (often accounting for one-quarter of government expenditure) but in producing both an escalation of, and an obsession with, educational credentials. This obsession has contributed to the undermining of the educational process – a veritable 'diploma disease' (see Shils, 1972, p. 25 on the effects of this in India). And besides this, the middle classes have had highly diverse effects upon the state and its role in modernisation. In certain cases, especially in Latin America, they have restricted the growth of the state, bolstered the traditional ruling bloc and prevented modernisation (see Nun, 1967, on their use of military coups) – while in parts of South-East Asia they have much more openly used the state and extended state employment in order to effect reform (see Wertheim, 1959).

However, for all these difficulties there are very significant consequences which stem from the growth of a strong middle class. We can reformulate Lewis and Maude's argument as to some of the political effects as follows.

The persistence of the middle classes in Britain can be in part explained in terms of their function in preventing the domination of any single element of social life, i.e. by capitalists, or state bureaucrats, or professionals. The effects on working-class politics are:

(*a*)   To obscure the overall domination of capitalist relations,
(*b*)   to provide 'professional', 'technical' legitimation of the overall society,
(*c*)   to provide leadership of working-class movements,
(*d*)   to prevent political domination by any one segment which would more obviously threaten working-class interests.

So there is a functional circle: the persistence but not the origin of the middle classes in Britain is partly explained in terms of its effect, particularly on displacing, leading and redirecting working-class struggle. As a consequence, the middle classes are strengthened, through benefiting economically from their performance of functions related to capital, through employment as working-class organisers, and through the mutually beneficial interdependence of capitalist, professional and state interests.

So far, then, we have suggested that this 'functionalist' literature poses important questions which indicate the virtues of analysing the critical interdependence of social classes and other social forces. In particular, the development of a large middle class may transform labourist politics and part of the explanation of the further development of the middle class is in terms of these functional consequences. (See Crossick, 1977a, pp. 48–50, for the view that the growth of white-collar workers before 1914 reinforced working-class unity.) However, in order to clarify these relationships further it is necessary to dispense with these 'functionalist' presuppositions. We will begin by considering an obviously dysfunctional process – namely, inflation.

Goldthorpe argues that the generally rising rate of inflation reflects a situation in which conflict between social groups and strata has become both more intense and more evenly matched. This has occurred in Britain because of three related developments. First, there has been a decay of the existing status order and an increased willingness to exploit one's market position – this results from the break-up of local 'interactional' status systems, the growth of commercialisation, and an increasing doubt and controversy over the actual bases of status attribution. Secondly, members of most social groupings have become citizens. Individuals have been seen to possess a set of civil, political and social rights which are relatively independent of market considerations and which will be strongly defended if threatened by, for example, redundancy. And thirdly, there is the emergence of a mature, industrialised and urbanised working class which is increasingly self-recruited (see Goldthorpe, 1978, p. 206, as well as 1980b), and which has enjoyed a marked continuity uninterrupted by dictatorship, internal war, or enemy occupation. Goldthorpe maintains:

The existence of trade unions and of a labour movement is an established fact of life, and for [the workers] ... trade unionism ... is the normal mode of action by which conditions of work and standards of living are to be defended and ... improved. (1978, p. 207)

In other words, in the UK monological organisations of labour are the normal means for resolving pay disputes, and in particular a mature working class is increasingly willing to engage in industrial and political actions against employers and the state.

Goldthorpe illustrates well the virtues of a 'sociological' understanding of inflation. However, he only considers the effects of the growth of the middle classes in two limited respects: (*a*) in helping to produce the increasingly self-recruited nature of the *mature* working class, and (*b*) in suggesting that white-collar workers may use the same means (that is, unions) in order to preserve pay differentials *vis-à-vis* workers. However, there are some further consequences that should be considered. In order to explore these we shall briefly consider Dahrendorf's recent analysis of contemporary politics (1980). He points out that there have been three crucial developments: (1) the new radicalism of the left, including the demands for participation and decentralisation; (2) the new radicalism of the right, including the return to law and order, discipline, individual responsibility and less taxation; (3) environmentalist and counter-cultural politics. In each case Dahrendorf argues that these forms of politics have emerged from the 'middle class', or what we have termed the 'service class': 'They are, in fact, the politics of teachers, of estate agents, and of students. What they show above all is a massive disorientation of the most numerous stratum of modern societies, the employed middle classes' (p. 7).

The development of the middle class has therefore generated new forms of politics and these in turn have affected ongoing practices in two respects. First, they have influenced existing political forces – Dahrendorf suggests that a new 'educational class' has emerged and it is this which is systematically taking over Western socialist parties. The effects of this are in part uncertain but it has certainly sustained a degree of socialist militance and organisation that would otherwise not have occurred (see Forester, 1976, and Hindess, 1971, for contrasting views on the British Labour Party). Secondly, according to Dahrendorf, it produces a general increase in the ambiguity of social relations, so that many people are, for example, in favour of large bureaucracies yet resentful of their increased power; or they are members of trade unions yet want their powers to be reduced. This produces a great increase in political uncertainty and instability which is reflected in the UK in an increasingly instrumental attitude to political parties, and in an overall decline in the class alignment of the major political parties. As Crewe *et al.* say even of the early 1970s (well before the founding of the SDP):

The decay in the class alignment was due almost entirely to the expansion of the Labour middle class ... Not for twenty years – perhaps more – had the middle classes displayed less partisan solidarity than the working class. (1977, pp. 169–70)

Dahrendorf thus suggests that although we live in a class society the classes of labour and capital have only a limited claim on people's commitment and, to some extent, both labour and capital can lay claim to the same members. We would argue that the recent period in the UK has been one in which the causal powers of the service class in particular have been considerably augmented, although we would also agree with Goldthorpe among others that there is fragmentation among the members of that class partly because of the particular patterns of recruitment into it (or at least classes 1 and 2 in Goldthorpe's schema; see 1980b, p. 270).

To return to the sociological analysis of inflation, we can extend and elaborate certain of Dahrendorf's claims as follows:

(1)   The socialisation of unproductive labour means that the social forces 'opposed' to capital have been further strengthened and this makes it difficult for capital to maintain the rate of exploitation.

(2)   This socialisation in turn means an extended elaboration of civil society and its horizontal rather than vertical reorganisation – and this means that there is a considerable growth in the number and diversity of social groupings which will mobilise to pursue their short-term interests. This includes both 'class' and 'popular democratic' groupings.

(3)   Many groupings will so mobilise although their struggles will often be directed against other middle-class organisations, and especially against the 'service class', rather than against an unambiguous 'dominant class'. There is a diversity of 'main enemies' against whom struggles will take place.

(4)   The effects of 1, 2 and 3 will be to extend the size and power of the state, since each grouping will increasingly feel that it can expect 'rising entitlements' (see Bell, 1979, p. 233). The service class, in particular, is generally the recipient of much welfare state provisions, especially in education, housing and health care (see Gould, 1980).

(5)   However, the form that state provision will take, bureaucratic, non-participatory and individualistic, may fail to satisfy such groupings, although it will provide many with employment. As a result of the form taken by state provision there will be further struggles, both to extend such provision and to achieve other improvements outside the state (community care, for example), with the result that civil society is further developed and more demands are made on capital.

(6)   Working-class organisations will respond to these developments (in

part, of course, they contribute to them) by further attempts to protect their short-term material interests and to reduce differentials with the service class.

(7) The heightened conflict between working-class organisations and these generated within the middle classes means that monological forms are generalised – which increases short-term pressures on the state to provide rising entitlements for each instrumentally operating social grouping.

(8) The increasing crises of capitalism reduce profits as a tax base and this heightens the inflationary pressure and the tendency to 'fiscal crisis' (see Jessop, 1980, on the British state and its fiscal crisis).

We now return to topics already touched on in Chapters 5 and 6 – namely, the place of professions within contemporary capitalism and the forms of knowledge upon which their power is based.

We can begin by briefly considering Gramsci's discussion of organic intellectuals. Clearly there is a major shift in the organic nature of such intellectuals with the socialisation of unproductive labour. As Gramsci says more generally, the relationship between intellectuals and the world of production 'is not as direct as it is with the fundamental social groups but is, in varying degrees, "mediated" by the whole fabric of society and by the complex of superstructures, of which the intellectuals are, precisely, the "functionaries"' (1971, p. 12). Such 'intellectuals' are located in part at least within civil society – a sphere within which relatively free association between approximate equals can take place. Thus, with the socialisation of unproductive labour there are a number of shifts: first, a decline in the significance of traditional intellectuals and hence a reduced ability to develop notions of disembodied or pure knowledge (see the discussion in Sassoon, 1980, pp. 134–46); secondly, a large increase in the size and complexity of the service class, in part generated by and within civil society; and thirdly, increased difficulties for the capitalist class to control their own service class, or 'organic intellectuals' – partly because of their constitution as associations of 'free persons' (see Parry and Parry, 1976, p. 264) who can to some degree generate and regulate their own forms of knowledge, albeit mediated by the state.

On the one hand, Marxists have been right to emphasise the increase in the degree to which professionals function for capital, as constitutive elements of the service class; yet on the other hand, Weberians have been correct to emphasise the distinctive market position of professionals which stems in part from their ability to regulate their particular knowledge-base. Larson maintains that the market situation of the modern profession depends upon effecting a structural linkage between two sets of elements: specific bodies of theoretical knowledge, on the one hand, and markets for skilled services or labour, on the other (see Larson, 1980, pp. 141–2; and 1977, more generally). This, she maintains, could only be achieved through the modern university which has connected together the production of increasingly esoteric knowledge with the standardised production of professional producers (see 1977, pp. 17, 51f.). This provided the basis for both claiming and sustaining the backing of the state for the monopoly of expertise – and this, once obtained, has provided a proven means of protection against more state interference (see p. 53). Larson convincingly shows how different occupational groupings have been organised as 'professions' in order to attain market power. Professionalisation she sees as 'the process by which producers of special services sought to constitute *and control* a market of their expertise'; but, at the same time, it is a 'collective assertion of special social status and a collective process of upward social mobility' (p. xvi). As a consequence, the very process of professionalisation has contributed to the restructuring of the patterning of social inequality, to a system based on the salience of occupation, to legitimation via achievement of socially recognised expertise, and to a concentration upon education and credentialling. Thus, the organisation of professional markets has had crucial consequences upon existing forms of structured social inequality, particularly upon the relations between labour and capital.

Larson demonstrates the crucial role of the university in unifying the production of knowledge with the production of the producers which has had the effect of enabling certain 'professions' to expand and to restructure existing social relations. Hence, the very form of capitalist development within a given society depends upon the degree to which existing or new occupations can be professionalised (see pp. 47–8 for some of the relevant factors involved). It also depends upon which occupations are professionalised and hence which sectors of the education system are developed.

For the USA Noble shows the importance of the growth of engineers, that is, of a profession directly incorporated into the production of surplus-value, by contrast, say, with medicine or law where the use-value is consumed partly independently of capitalist relations of production (see Noble, 1979, as well as Larson, 1977, pp. 213–19). Noble demonstrates that the profession of modern engineering was from the very beginning in the USA (1860s onwards) integrated with that of corporate capital, even to the extent of attempting to foster appropriate working practices and social habits among the labour force. Professional engineers were highly influential in effecting a number of major changes in the USA in the period 1860–1930: standardising weights and measurement, modernising patent law in favour of the science-based industrial corporations, developing large industrial research laboratories, integrating industrial and university-based research, ensuring an appropriate industry-based curriculum within the dramatically expanding university system, and helping to produce modern management and its techniques of overcoming workers' resistance (see Noble, 1979, pt 2).

Three important consequences thus stem from the organisation of professional engineers within the USA. First, they in part produced the divorce between mental and manual labour itself and thus enlarged the size, effectivity and ultimately the differentiation of mental workers; in other words, their struggle in part transformed the existing class structure (see Kocka, 1980, for details). Stark notes that the engineering profession in the USA increased from 7,000 in 1880 to 136,000 in 1920; however, 'the occupants of the new positions did not simply "fill in" a set of "empty places" created by forces completely divorced from their own activity, but actually participated, within a constellation of struggling classes, in the creation of these positions themselves' (1980, p. 101). It is interesting to note that British development was much less advanced. In 1911 the *Engineer* had objected to scientific management with the comment that 'there are fair ways and unfair ways of diminishing labour costs . . . We do not hesitate to say that Taylorism is inhuman' (quoted in Wiener, 1981, p. 143; see Roderick and Stephens, 1981, on the development of engineering within the British university system). Secondly, as Noble argues:

In emphasising the role of formal education as a vital aspect of their professional identity, they [professional engineers] at the same time laid the groundwork for the education-based occupational stratification of twentieth-century corporate America. (1979, p. 168)

The existence of a relatively small but increasingly wealthy and powerful grouping served to exacerbate the demand for substantial opportunities to acquire such positions, in other words, that there should be widely diffused educational opportunities, especially to obtain a college degree. The demand for mass higher education helped both to produce a reserve army of qualified mental workers and to escalate the level of qualifications appropriate for any particular place within the social division of labour (see Collins, 1977, p. 131). And thirdly, the engineers provided a model of how education and industry were to be integrated over the course of the twentieth century as one occupation after another sought to strengthen its market-power by connecting together the production of knowledge with the production of the producers via the modern university. This has been true both of occupations within the spheres of production/circulation and within civil society and the state, where part of the expansion of each can be seen to result from the strategy of professionalisation. It is interesting to note that in the UK universities have, until fairly recently, been less centrally involved in the processes of collective social mobility of newly emergent occupational groupings, especially those within the economy (see Wiener, 1981, generally on the 'gentrification of the industrialist' in the UK, and pp. 132—7 in particular on universities and industry; and see Sanderson, 1972).

Finally, we shall consider very briefly what the political consequences are of this linking together of the profession and the university, of the existence of a service class which is distinguished from deskilled white-collar workers particularly in terms of the superior educational credentials required to enter such places (which go together with a superior work situation).

(1)   Since, as Foucault and others have shown, power is increasingly based on knowledge, challenging relations of power necessarily involves the acquisition of knowledge, and that progressively means working through channels of formal education (on the power/knowledge relationship see Foucault, 1980). Yet that in turn involves the acquisition of educational credentials which in part serve to separate labour off both from the service class and to some extent from deskilled white-collar workers. Hence the paradox that challenging power requires knowledge, yet the acquisition of that knowledge is organised so that it reinforces the very credentially based system of power that is in part the original object of contestation.

(2)   This system is, moreover, made to seem legitimate precisely because many such places are acquired as a consequence of achieved educational credentials. As Larson says of professionals in the USA, 'They seem to have, more importantly than income, a claim to dignity and respect. This claim appears *to be formed entirely on superior education*' (1977, p. 242; original emphasis). The professions have established and sustained many of the links between education and the labour market; they reinforce the notion that rewards are rationally distributed to the ablest and hardest-striving. Hence, they hold out to labour the attractions of individual achievement and the costs of class as opposed to associational or professional actions.

(3)   The social and political implications of the growth of a service class somewhat separate from capital have produced a substantial radicalisation within such occupations. This has been termed the 'radicals in the professions' movement which challenges both the internal organisation of professions and the effects that these professions have on the overall society (see Perucci, 1973; and above, p. 79ff). Hence, a major consequence of the growth of the service class through educational expansion has been to generate radicalisation within that class at the place of work.

(4)   This has spilled over to more widespread generation of oppositional 'fragments' of various forms of community, ecological, consumerist, cultural, sexual and local politics (see, for example, Rowbotham *et al.*, 1980; and the Leninist critique in Goodwin, 1980). These fragments are normally characterised as 'middle class'. Goodwin argues:

This relatively privileged minority not only finds itself separated from the rest of the working class by culture and tradition. It is also, by virtue of its relatively privileged social position, particularly pressured in its politics towards ghettoisation and retreat into 'life style'. (1980, p.98)

However, Goodwin seems to imagine that simply inveighing against these fragments will be sufficient to make them disappear. Our argument, by contrast, is that contemporary politics has been transformed by the massive development of the 'educated' classes and the partial realisation of their causal powers. These fragments (however 'ghettoised' and 'lifestyle-oriented') will be a consistently significant feature of such politics. The struggles of labour are thus transformed by, first, being removed from the centre of the historical stage; secondly, having the service class as their apparent 'main enemy' over numbers of issues; and thirdly, through sections of that service class developing alternative political forms which 'out-radicalise' labour (feminist and ecological politics are the best examples).

(5) As a consequence, labour cannot avoid seeking allies within the educated classes, whether they practise electoralism or non-electoral revolutionary politics. (This is convincingly shown in Przeworski, 1977; and see Hales, 1980, p. 109.) This is not a new dilemma for labour (and for socialist politics) – after all, when Engels claimed in 1895 that socialists would become a force before which 'all powers will have to bow' this was in fact conditional upon their success in 'conquering the greater part of the middle strata of society' (quoted in Przeworski, 1980, p. 40). However, it is noteworthy that if anything the conquering is now taking place the other way round. So although it is incorrect to see the service class as a potential ruling class, as Gouldner predicts for his 'new class' (1979), it does have substantial causal powers, to generate its own horizontal organisations and to disaggregate civil society, and these will increasingly frustrate the realisation of the powers of the proletariat. So, although the socialisation of unproductive labour has generated a large number of deskilled and in part 'proletarianised' white-collar workers, the social context within which this has taken place is one in which there is a substantial increase in the realisation of the powers of the service class. The development of their power has been at the expense of both capital and, especially, labour. As Gould says of the conceptually similar 'salaried middle class', its interests 'are effectively advanced with limited class organization, visibility and consciousness . . . it has assumed a high degree of power without capital, labour or itself recognising what has taken place; and . . . its role in welfare and corporatist politics has been neglected and underestimated' (1980, p. 416).

Conclusion

In working towards an account of the positions of the middle classes in contemporary capitalist societies, we have had several aims in mind. First, we have argued that a separation of Marxist and Weberian theory is not now theoretically profitable and that an adequate theory may well seem eclectic, incorporating and rejecting elements of both approaches. Secondly, any consideration of the position of these groups, apparently situated between labour and capital, has to recognise the crucial difference between what we have called the service class and deskilled white-collar workers. Thirdly, an understanding of the development of socialised unproductive labour is essential for an appreciation of the relationship of these two groups with each other, and with the working class. Fourthly, any theory of class must not rigidly separate class determination from class struggle, since the effects of the latter enter into the very structures that determine class places. Furthermore, the recruitment of people into such places vitally affects the realisation of the causal powers of social classes.

(1) In Part One of this book we reviewed a body of theory and evidence concerning the middle classes. This review provided much of the material with which we have discussed certain issues in Part Two, but it also indicated the difficulties of adequately separating Marxist and Weberian theory. As a result of this discussion, we argued in Part Two that social classes should be (a) seen as sets of social relations connecting together places within the social division of labour, (b) conceptualised in terms of market and work situations, and (c) seen as involving important processes of recruitment which in part affect the structuring of such places.

Furthermore, it is impossible to account for the generation of class places, seen in this way, without also understanding the functions which such places perform, functions which can only be interpreted in terms of a theory of capitalist development. We are therefore proposing an analysis at three very closely connected levels: the development of capitalist social relations, the assignment of capitalist functions to class places, and the relationship of functions to market and work situations.

(2) We have argued that, applying this analysis to the position of the middle classes in British society, there are different market and work situations, and hence class positions, of the service class and of deskilled white-collar workers. Underlying this distinction is an increasing functional

separation, whereby the service class is taking on, and concentrating within itself, the functions of capital, namely, conceptualisation, control, and reproduction. The white-collar labour process is simultaneously becoming deskilled, siphoning capital functions up into the service class, while proletarianising the deskilled white-collar workers, who cannot, therefore, be properly be seen as a 'middle class'. But also, in an important sense, neither can the service class. As we have said, in this class are concentrated the functions of control, conceptualisation and reproduction, functions delegated from capital and, historically speaking, from the capitalist class. Because of the depersonalisation of property ownership, the distinctive market and work situation and hence class position of the capitalist class is being transformed, and its functions are becoming somewhat indistinguishable from those of the service class.

(3) We have argued that a new and relatively unrecognised process within the development of capitalism is the socialisation of unproductive labour. This is not a uniform process affecting the service class and deskilled white-collar workers equally, since capital functions are not evenly distributed across the two groups. This uneven distribution is most clearly seen in the separation of mental from manual labour and in the development of educated labour, features progressively concentrated in the service class and reinforced by the tendency to attach demands for specific credentials to places within the service class. Because of the transformed relationship of labour and knowledge in contemporary capitalism, places within the social division of labour are crucially structured by different educational requirements; in particular, white-collar places are distinguished from the service class in terms of the differences in credentials demanded. And, at the same time, the process of class formation, of the recruitment of persons to places, is increasingly the outcome of the distribution of hierarchically ordered educational credentials to such persons.

(4) None of these processes, however, is to be viewed as determined directly by economic laws. We have argued strongly that the process by which knowledge is reorganised into highly separated mental and manual labours involves intense class struggle. More generally, we have argued that classes are to be seen as possessing powers to produce empirical outcomes. And in particular, we have maintained that in modern capitalist societies the 'causal powers' of the service class have become significantly enhanced – powers reflected in various kinds of economic, political and social struggles which have increased the development of the socialisation of unproductive labour, forced mental and manual labour further apart, increased the credentialisation of both places and persons, concentrated capital functions within the service class, deskilled the white-collar labour process, separated the service class from deskilled white-collar workers in respect of their market and work situations, and transformed the political position of labour. They have, in other words, transformed the very structure within which the service class is to be seen as a 'class-in-struggle'.

Analysing social classes in terms of potentially realisable causal powers both dispenses with the relatively trivial Boundary Problem and indicates that contemporary capitalist societies will vary considerably in the forms and patterns of stratification displayed. Our general claim that the service class is a relatively powerful entity in modern capitalism should not conceal the historical and comparative variations identifiable, especially resulting from the particular forms of both civil society and the state. Another book would attempt to explain such variations and to analyse in detail the substantial implications for labour within different late capitalist societies.

Bibliography

Abercrombie, N. (1980), *Class, Structure and Knowledge* (Oxford: Blackwell).

Abercrombie, N., Hill, S. R., and Turner, B. (1980), *The Dominant Ideology Thesis* (London: Allen & Unwin).

Albert, M., and Hahnel, R. (1979), 'A ticket to ride: more locations on the class map', in Walker (ed.), op. cit., pp. 243–78.

Anderson, G. (1976), *Victorian Clerks* (Manchester: Manchester University Press).

Anderson, G. (1977), 'The social economy of late-Victorian clerks', in Crossick (ed.), op. cit., pp. 113–33.

APEX (1980), 'A trade union strategy for the new technology', in Forester (ed.), op. cit., pp. 374–90.

Aristotle (1962), *Politics* (Harmondsworth: Penguin).

Arnold, M. (1964), ed. R. H. Super, *Schools and Universities on the Continent* (Ann Arbor, Mich.: Michigan University Press).

Babbage, C. (1832), *On the Economy of Machinery and Manufactures* (London: Knight).

Bain, G. S. (1970), *The Growth of White Collar Unionism* (London: Oxford University Press).

Bain, G. S., and Price, R. (1972), 'Who is a white-collar employee?', *British Journal of Industrial Relations*, vol. 10, pp. 325–39.

Bain, G. S., Coates, D., and Ellis, V. (1973), *Social Stratification and Trade Unionism* (London: Heinemann).

Balibar, E. (1977), *On the Dictatorship of the Proletariat* (London: New Left Books).

Bamber, G., Glover, J., and Hall, K. (1975), 'Proletarianisation of managers and technical specialists in industrial society?', paper presented to the British Sociological Association annual conference, March.

Baran, P., and Sweezy, P. (1968), *Monopoly Capital* (Harmondsworth: Penguin).

Baudelot, C., Establet, R., and Malemort, J. (1974), *La Petite Bourgeoisie en France* (Paris: Maspéro).

Bechhofer, F., and Elliott, B. (1968), 'An approach to a study of small shopkeepers and the class structure', *European Journal of Sociology*, vol. 9, pp. 180–202.

Bechhofer, F., Elliott, B., Rushforth, M., and Bland, R. (1974a), 'Small shopkeepers; matters of meaning and money', *Sociological Review*, vol. 22, pp. 465–82.

Bechhofer, F., Elliott, B., Rushforth, M., and Bland, R. (1974b), 'The petit bourgeoisie in the class structure', in *The Social Analysis of the Class Structure*, ed. F. Parkin (London: Tavistock), pp. 103–28.

Bechhofer, F., and Elliott, B. (1976), 'Persistence and change; the petit bourgeoisie in industrial society', *European Journal of Sociology*, vol. 17, pp. 74–99.

Bechhofer, F., Elliott, B., and McCrone, D. (1978), 'Structure, consciousness, and action', *British Journal of Sociology*, vol. 29, pp. 410–36.
Bell, C. (1968), *Middle Class Families* (London: Routledge & Kegan Paul).
Bell, D. (1974), *The Coming of Post Industrial Society* (London: Heinemann).
Bell, D. (1979), *The Cultural Contradictions of Capitalism* (London: Heinemann).
Bendix, R. (1956), *Work and Authority in Industry* (New York: Wiley).
Benson, L. (1978), *Proletarians and Parties* (London: Tavistock).
Berg, I. (1970), *Education and Jobs: The Great Training Robbery* (New York: Praeger).
Bernstein, E. (1961), *Evolutionary Socialism* (New York: Schocken).
Blackbourn, D. (1977), 'The *Mittelstand* in German society and politics, 1871–1914', *Social History*, no. 4, pp. 409–33.
Blackburn, R. M. (1967), *Union Character and Social Class* (London: Batsford).
Blackburn, R. M., and Mann, M. (1979), *The Working Class in the Labour Market* (London: Macmillan).
Blackburn, R. M., and Prandy, K. (1965), 'White-collar unionisation: a conceptual framework', *British Journal of Sociology*, vol. 16, pp. 111–21.
Blain, A. N. J. (1972), *Pilots and Management* (London: Allen & Unwin).
Bott, E. (1957), *Family and Social Network* (London: Tavistock).
Bottomore, T. B. (1965), *Classes in Modern Society* (London: Allen & Unwin).
Bottomore, T., and Goode, P. (eds and translators) (1978), *Austro-Marxism* (Oxford: Clarendon Press).
Bouchier, D. (1978), *Idealism and Revolution* (London: Edward Arnold).
Bradley, I. (1975), 'The question mark over the future of the middle classes', *The Times*, 7 January.
Braverman, H. (1974), *Labour and Monopoly Capital* (New York: Monthly Review Press).
Braverman, H. (1976), 'Two comments', *Monthly Review*, vol. 28, pp. 119–25.
Brown, A. (1936), *The Fate of the Middle Classes* (London: Gollancz).
Buck, T. (1979), 'Regional class differences', *International Journal of Urban and Regional Research*, vol. 3, pp. 516–26.
Buck, T., and Atkins, M. (1978), 'Social class and spatial problems', *Town Planning Review*, vol. 49, pp. 209–21.
Burawoy, M. (1978), 'Towards a Marxist theory of the Labour process: Braverman and beyond', *Politics and Society*, vols 3–4, pp. 247–312.
Burawoy, M. (1979), *Manufacturing Consent* (Chicago: Chicago University Press).
Burns, J. C. (1980), 'The automated office', in Forester (ed.), op. cit., pp. 220–31.
Carchedi, G. (1977), *On the Economic Identification of Social Classes* (London: Routledge & Kegan Paul).
Carrillo, S. (1977), *'Eurocommunism' and the State* (London: Lawrence & Wishart).
Chandler, A. (1977), *The Visible Hand* (Cambridge, Mass.: Harvard University Press).
Clawson, D. (1980), *Bureaucracy and the Labour Process* (New York: Monthly Review Press).
Clements, R. V. (1958), *Managers: A Study of their Careers in Industry* (London: Allen & Unwin).
Cole, G. D. H. (1950), 'The conception of the middle classes', *British Journal of Sociology*, vol. 1, pp. 275–90.

Collins, R. (1977), 'Functional and conflict theories of educational stratification', in *Power and Ideology in Education*, ed. J. Karabel and A. H. Halsey (New York: Oxford University Press), pp. 118–36.

Cooke, P. (1980), 'Dependency formation and modes of integration: the historical and contemporary case of Wales', University of Wales Institute of Science and Technology, Cardiff, mimeo.

Cooley, M. J. E. (1977), 'Taylor in the office', in *Humanising the Workplace*, ed. R. N. Ottoway (London: Croom Helm).

Corey, L. (1935), *The Crisis of the Middle Class* (Cevici Friede).

Crewe, I., Särlvik, B., and Alt, J. (1977), 'Partisan alignment in Britain, 1964–1974', *British Journal of Political Science*, vol. 7, pp. 129–90.

Crompton, R. (1976), 'Approaches to the study of white-collar unionism', *Sociology*, vol. 10, pp. 407–26.

Crompton, R. (1979), 'Trade unionism and the insurance clerk', *Sociology*, vol. 13, pp. 403–26.

Crompton, R. (1980), 'Class mobility in modern Britain', *Sociology*, vol. 14, pp. 117–19.

Crompton, R., and Gubbay, J. (1977), *Economy and Class Structure* (London: Macmillan).

Crompton, R., and Jones, G. (1981), 'Clerical "proletarianisation": myth or reality', paper presented to the British Sociological Association annual conference.

Croner, F. (1954), 'Salaried employees in modern society', *International Labour Review*, vol. 69, pp. 97–110.

Crossick, G. (1977a), 'The emergence of the lower middle class in Britain: a discussion', in Crossick (ed.), op. cit., pp. 11–60.

Crossick, G. (ed.) (1977b), *The Lower Middle Class in Britain* (London: Croom Helm).

Crozier, M. (1965), *The World of the Office Worker* (Chicago: Chicago University Press).

CSE Microelectronics Group (1980), *Microelectronics: Capitalist Technology and the Working Class* (London: CSE Books).

Cutler, A., Hindess, B., Hirst, P., and Hussain, A. (1977), *Marx's Capital and Capitalism Today* (London: Routledge & Kegan Paul).

Cutler, A. (1978), 'The romance of "labour"', *Economy and Society*, vol. 7, pp. 74–95.

Dahrendorf, R. (1959), *Class and Class Conflict in an Industrial Society* (London: Routledge & Kegan Paul).

Dahrendorf, R. (1967), *Conflict after Class: New Perspectives on the Theory of Social and Political Conflict* (London: Longman).

Dahrendorf, R. (1969), 'The service class', in *Industrial Man*, ed. T. Burns (Harmondsworth: Penguin), pp. 140–50.

Dahrendorf, R. (1979), *Life Chances* (London: Weidenfeld & Nicolson).

Dahrendorf, R. (1980), 'The collapse of class spawns a new politics', *Guardian*, 15 September.

Dale, J. R. (1962), *The Clerk in Industry* (Liverpool: Liverpool University Press).

Davies, M. (1974), 'Women's place is at the typewriter: the feminisation of the clerical work force', *Radical America*, vol. 8, pp. 1–38.

Debray, R. (1981), *Teachers, Writers, Celebrities* (London: Verso).

De Kadt, M. (1979), 'Insurance: a clerical work factory', in *Case Studies on the*

Labour Process, ed. A. Zimbalist (New York: Monthly Review Press), pp. 242–56.

Delgado, A. (1979), *The Enormous File* (London: John Murray).

De Tocqueville, A. (1966), *Democracy in America*, Vol. 2 (New York: Harper & Row).

Dore, R. (1976), *The Diploma Disease* (London: Allen & Unwin).

Downing, H. (1980), 'Word processors and the oppression of women', in Forester, 1980, pp. 275–87.

Drabble, M. (1977), *The Ice Age* (London: Weidenfeld & Nicolson).

Duncan, M. (1981), 'Microelectronics: five areas of subordination', in *Science, Technology and the Labour Process*, ed. L. Levidow and B. Young (London: CSE Books), pp. 172–207.

Dunleavy, P. (1980), 'The political implications of sectoral cleavages and the growth of state employment. Part I: The analysis of production cleavages', *Political Studies*, vol. 28, pp. 370–83.

Earl, M. J. (1980), 'What micros mean for managers', in Forester (ed.), op. cit., pp. 220–31.

'EDP Analyzer' (1980), 'The experience of word processing', in Forester (ed.), op. cit., pp. 232–43.

Edwards, R. C. (1978), 'The social relations of production at the point of production', *Insurgent Sociologist*, vol. 8, pp. 109–25.

Edwards, R. C. (1979), *Contested Terrain* (London: Heinemann).

Ehrenreich, B., and Ehrenreich, J. (1979a), 'The professional-managerial class' in Walker (ed.). op. cit., pp. 5–45.

Ehrenreich, B., and Ehrenreich, J. (1979b), 'Rejoinder', in Walker (ed.), op. cit., pp. 313–34.

Eichler, M. (1980), *The Double Standard* (London: Croom Helm).

Elger, T. (1979), 'Valorisation and "deskilling": a critique of Braverman', *Capital and Class*, vol. 7, pp. 59–99.

Fidler, J. (1981), *The British Business Elite* (London: Routledge & Kegan Paul).

Forester, T. (1976), *The Labour Party and the Working Class* (London: Heinemann).

Forester, T. (ed.) (1980), *The Microelectronics Revolution* (Oxford: Blackwell).

Foucault, M. (1980), *Power/Knowledge: Selected Interviews and Other Writings 1972–1977*, ed. C. Gordon (Hassocks: Harvester).

Fraser, R. (ed.) (1968) *Work*, Vol. 1 (London: Penguin/New Left Books).

Fraser, R. (ed.) (1969), *Work*, Vol. 2 (London: Penguin/New Left Books).

Freedman, F. (1975), 'The internal structure of the American proletariat: a Marxist analysis', *Socialist Revolution*, vol. 26, pp. 41–84.

Freeman, R. (1976), *The Overeducated American* (New York: Academic Press).

Friedman, A. (1977a), *Industry and Labour* (London: Macmillan).

Friedman, A. (1977b), 'Responsible autonomy versus direct control over the labour process', *Capital and Class*, vol. I, pp. 43–57.

Friedson, E. (1973), 'Professionalisation and the organisation of middle-class labour in postindustrial society', in *Professionalisation and Social Change*, ed. P. Holmes, Sociological Review Monograph No. 20 (Keele: University of Kent), pp. 47–59.

Fröbel, F., Heinrichs, J., and Kreye, O. (1980), *The New International Division of Labour* (Cambridge: Cambridge University Press).

Gamble, A., and Walton, P. (1976), *Capitalism in Crisis: Inflation and the State* (London: Macmillan).

Garnsey, E. (1978), 'Women's work and theories of class stratification', *Sociology*, vol. 12, pp. 223–43.

Garrard, J., Jary, D., Goldsmith, M., and Oldfield, A. (eds) (1979), *The Middle Classes in Politics* (Farnborough: Saxon House).

Gershuny, J. (1978), *After Industrial Society* (London: Macmillan).

Gershuny, J., and Pahl, R. (1979), 'Work outside employment: some preliminary speculations', *New Universities Quarterly*, vol. 34, pp. 120–35.

Giddens, A. (1973), *The Class Structure of the Advanced Societies* (London: Hutchinson).

Giddens, A. (1980), 'Classes, capitalism and the state', *Theory and Society*, vol. 9, pp. 877–90.

Glenn, E. N., and Feldberg, R. L. (1979), 'Proletarianizing clerical work; technology and organisational control in the office', in *Case Studies on the Labour Process*, ed. A. Zimbalist (New York: Monthly Review Press), pp. 51–72.

Goldthorpe, J. H. (1972), 'Class, status and party in modern Britain: some recent interpretations, Marxist and Marxisant', *European Journal of Sociology*, vol. 13, pp. 342–72.

Goldthorpe, J. H. (1978), 'The current inflation: towards a sociological account', in *The Political Economy of Inflation*, ed. F. Hirsch and J. Goldthorpe (Oxford: Martin Robertson), pp. 186–214.

Goldthorpe, J. H. (1980a), 'Reply to Crompton', *Sociology*, vol. 14, pp. 121–23.

Goldthorpe, J. H. (1980b), *Social Mobility and Class Structure in Modern Britain* (Oxford: Clarendon Press).

Goldthorpe, J. H., Lockwood, D., Bechhofer, F., and Platt, J. (1969), *The Affluent Worker in the Class Structure* (Cambridge: Cambridge University Press).

Goodrich, C. L. (1920), *The Frontier of Control* (London: Bell).

Goodwin, P. (1980), 'Beyond the fragments', *International Socialism*, 2nd ser., no. 9, pp. 95–117.

Gordon, D., Edwards, R. C., and Reich, M. (1975), *Labour Market Segmentation* (Lexington, Mass.: D. C. Heath).

Gorz, A. (1967), *Strategy for Labour* (Boston, Mass.: Beacon Press).

Gorz, A. (1976), 'Technology, technicians and class struggle', in *The Division of Labour*, ed. A. Gorz (Hassocks: Harvester), pp. 159–89.

Gould, A. (1980), 'The salaried middle class in the corporatist welfare state', *Policy and Politics*, vol. 9, pp. 401–18.

Gouldner, A. W. (1979), *The Future of Intellectuals and the Rise of the New Class* (London: Macmillan).

Gramsci, A. (1971), *Selections from the Prison Notebooks*, ed. Q. Hoare and P. Nowell Smith (London: Lawrence & Wishart).

Greenbaum, J. (1976), 'Division of labour in the computer field', *Monthly Review*, vol. 28, pp. 40–55.

Greenfield, H. I. (1966), *Manpower and the Growth of Producer Services* (New York: Columbia University Press).

Gross, L. (1949), 'The use of class concepts in sociological research', *American Journal of Sociology*, vol. 54, pp. 409–21.

Haber, S. (1964), *Efficiency and Uplift, Scientific Management in the Progressive Era, 1890–1920* (Chicago: Chicago University Press).

Hakim, C. (1979), *Occupational Segregation*, Research Paper No. 9, Department of Employment (London: HMSO).

Hales, M. (1980), *Living Thinkwork* (London: CSE Books).

Hall, J., and Caradog Jones, D. (1950), 'Social grading of occupations', *British Journal of Sociology*, vol. 1, pp. 31–55.

Hall, S. (1980), 'Nicos Poulantzas: state, power, socialism', *New Left Review*, vol. 19, pp. 60–9.

Halsey, A. H., Heath, A. F., and Ridge, J. M. (1980), *Origins and Destinations* (Oxford: Oxford University Press).

Harré, R., and Madden, E. (1975), *Causal Powers* (Oxford: Blackwell).

Harries-Jenkins, G. (1970), 'Professionals in organisations', in *Professions and Professionalisation*, ed. J. A. Jackson (Cambridge: Cambridge University Press), pp. 51–108.

Harris, A. (1939), 'Pure capitalism and the disappearance of the middle class', *Journal of Political Economy*, vol. 47, pp. 328–56.

Hartmann, H. (1979), 'Capitalism, patriarchy and job segregation by sex', in *Capitalist Patriarchy and the Case for Socialist Feminism*, ed. Z. Eisenstein (New York: Monthly Review Press), pp. 206–47.

Hatt, P. K. (1950), 'Occupation and social stratification', *American Journal of Sociology*, vol. 55, pp. 533–43.

Heap, S. H. (1980), 'World profitability crisis in the 1970s: some empirical evidence', *Capital and Class*, vol. 12, pp. 66–84.

Heath, A. (1981), *Social Mobility* (London: Fontana).

Henderson, P. (1976), 'Class structure and the concept of intelligence', in *Schooling and Capitalism*, ed. R. Dale *et al.* (Milton Keynes: Open University Press), pp. 142–51.

Heritage, J. (1980), 'Class situation, white collar unionisation and the "double proletarianisation" thesis: a comment', *Sociology*, vol. 14, pp. 283–94.

Hill, S. (1981), *Competition and Control at Work* (London: Heinemann).

Hindess, B. (1971), *The Decline of Working Class Politics* (London: MacGibbon & Kee).

Hindess, B. (1981), 'The politics of social mobility', *Economy and Society*, vol. 10, pp. 184–202.

Hirst, P. Q. (1977), 'Economic classes and politics', in *Class and Class Structure*, ed. A. Hunt (London: Lawrence & Wishart), pp. 125–54.

Hirst, P. Q. (1979), *On Law and Ideology* (London: Macmillan).

Hussain, A. (1976), 'The economy and the educational system in capitalist societies', *Economy and Society*, vol. 5, pp. 413–34.

Hutber, P. (1977), *The Decline and Fall of the Middle Class* (Harmondsworth: Penguin).

Hymer, R. (1975), 'The multinational corporation and the law of uneven development', in Radice (ed.), op. cit., pp. 37–62.

Jacoby, R. (1978), 'Political economy and class unconsciousness', *Theory and Society*, vol. 5, pp. 11–18.

Jamous, H., and Peloille, B. (1970), 'Changes in the French university-hospital system', in *Professions and Professionalisation*, ed. J. A. Jackson (Cambridge: Cambridge University Press), pp. 111–52.

Jessop, B. (1980), 'The transformation of the state in post-war Britain', in *The State in Western Europe*, ed. R. Scase (London: Croom Helm), pp. 23–93.

Johnson, C. (1980), 'The problem of reformism and Marx's theory of fetishism', *New Left Review*, vol. 119, pp. 70–96.

Johnson, T. (1972), *Professions and Power* (London: Macmillan).

Johnson, T. (1977a), 'The professions in the class structure', in *Industrial Society: Class, Cleavage and Control*, ed. R. Scase (London: Allen & Unwin), pp. 93–110.

Johnson, T. (1977b), 'What is to be known? The structural determination of class', *Economy and Society*, vol. 7, pp. 194–233.

Kapferer, N. (1980), 'Commodity, science and technology: a critique of Sohn-Rethel', in *Outlines of a Critique of Technology*, ed. P. Slater (London: Ink Links), pp. 74–95.

Kautsky, K. (1971), *The Class Struggle* (New York: Norton).

Keat, R., and Urry, J. (1982), *Social Theory as Science*, 2nd edn. (London: Routledge & Kegan Paul).

Kelly, M. P. (1980), *White-Collar Proletariat* (London: Routledge & Kegan Paul).

King, R., and Raynor, J. (1981), *The Middle Class* (London: Longman).

King, R., and Nugent, M. (eds) (1979), *Respectable Rebels* (London: Hodder & Stoughton).

Klingender, F. D. (1935), *The Condition of Clerical Labour in Britain* (London: Martin Lawrence).

Kocka, J. (1980), *White Collar Workers in America, 1890–1940* (London: Sage).

Kohn, M. L. (1971), 'Bureaucratic man: a portrait and an interpretation', *American Sociological Review*, vol. 36, pp. 461–74.

Kraft, P. (1979), 'The industrialisation of computer programming: from programming to "software production"', in *Case Studies on the Labour Process*, ed. A. Zimbalist (New York: Monthly Review Press), pp. 1–17.

Kreckel, R. (1980), 'Unequal opportunity structure and labour market segmentation', *Sociology*, vol. 14, pp. 525–50.

Laclau, E. (1979), *Politics and Ideology in Marxist Theory* (London: Verso).

Larkin, P. (1947), *A Girl in Winter* (London: Faber).

Larson, M. S. (1977), *The Rise of Professionalism: A Sociological Analysis* (Berkeley, Calif.: University of California Press).

Larson, M. S. (1980), 'Proletarianisation and educated labour', *Theory and Society*, vol. 9, pp. 131–75.

Lebovićs, E. (1969), *Social Conservatism and the Middle Classes in Germany, 1914–1933* (Princeton, NJ: Princeton University Press).

Lederer, E. (1912), *The Problem of the Modern Salaried Employee: Its Theoretical and Statistical Basis* (Tübingen).

Lee, C. H. (1979), *British Regional Employment Statistics, 1841–1971* (Cambridge: Cambridge University Press).

Leggatt, T. (1970), 'Teaching as a profession', in *Professions and Professionalisation*, ed. J. A. Jackson (Cambridge: Cambridge University Press), pp. 193–278.

Lewis, R., and Maude, A. (1949), *The English Middle Classes* (London: Phoenix House).

Littler, C. R. (1978), 'Understanding Taylorism', *British Journal of Sociology*, vol. 29, pp. 185–202.

Littler, C. R. (1982), *The Development of the Labour Process in Capitalist Societies* (London: Heinemann).

Lockwood, D. (1958), *The Blackcoated Worker* (London: Allen & Unwin).

Loveridge, R., and Mok, A. L. (1979), *Theories of Labour Market Segmentation* (The Hague: Martinus Nijhoff).

Lumley, R. (1973), *White Collar Unionism in Britain* (London: Methuen).

McCarthy, T. (1978), *Marx and the Proletariat* (London: Greenwood).
McClelland, D. (1961), *The Achieving Society* (New York: Van Nostrand).
McNally, F. (1979), *Women for Hire* (London: Macmillan).
Mallet, S. (1975), *Essays on the New Working Class* (St Louis, Missouri: Telos Press).
Mandel, E. (1975), *Late Capitalism* (London: New Left Books).
Marglin, S. (1974), 'What do bosses do?', in *The Division of Labour*, ed. A. Gorz (Hassocks: Harvester), pp. 13–54.
Marquand, J. (1980), *The Role of the Tertiary Sector in Regional Policy*, Regional Policy Series No. 19 (Brussels: Commission of the European Communities).
Marx, K. (1919a), *Theorien über den Mehrwert*, Vol. 1 (Stuttgart: Dietz).
Marx, K. (1919b), *Theorien über den Mehrwert*, Vol. 2 (Stuttgart: Dietz).
Marx, K. (1919c), *Theorien über den Mehrwert*, Vol. 3 (Stuttgart: Dietz).
Marx, K. (1959), *Capital*, Vol. 3 (London: Lawrence & Wishart).
Marx, K. (1976), *Capital*, Vol. 1 (Harmondsworth: Penguin).
Marx, K. (1978), *Capital*, Vol. 2 (Harmondsworth: Penguin).
Marx, K., and Engels, F. (1967), *Manifesto of the Communist Party* (Harmondsworth: Penguin).
Massey, D. (1981), 'The UK electrical engineering and electronics industries: the implications of the crisis for the restructuring of capital and locational change', in *Urbanisation and Urban Planning in Capitalist Society*, ed. M. Dear and A. J. Scott (London: Methuen), pp. 199–230.
Mills, C. W. (1951), *White Collar* (New York: Oxford University Press).
Minns, R. (1980), *Pension Funds and British Capitalism* (London: Heinemann).
Montgomery, D. (1979), *Workers' Control in America* (Cambridge: Cambridge University Press).
Morenco, C. (1965), 'Gradualism, apathy and suspicion in a French bank', in *Office Automation: Administrative and Human Problems*, ed. W. H. Scott (Paris: OECD).
Mulhern, F. (1981), ' "Teachers, writers, celebrities", intelligentsias and their histories', *New Left Review*, vol. 126, pp. 43–59.
Mumford, E., and Banks, O. (1967), *The Computer and the Clerk* (London: Routledge & Kegan Paul).
Mumford, E., and Ward, T. B. (1968), *Computers: Planning for People* (London: Batsford).
Murgatroyd, L. (1982), 'Gender and occupational stratification', Lancaster Regionalism Group, Working Paper No. 6.
Nelson, D. (1974), 'Scientific management, systematic management, and labor, 1880–1915', *Business History Review*, vol. 48, pp. 479–500.
Nelson, D. (1975), *Managers and Workers. Origins of the New Factory System in the United States, 1880–1920* (Madison, Wis.: University of Wisconsin Press).
Nelson, R. (1959), *The Merger Movement in American Industry 1895–1956* (Princeton, NJ: Princeton University Press).
Nicolaus, M. (1967), 'Proletariat and middle class in Marx: Hegelian choreography and the capitalist dialectic', *Studies on the Left*, vol. 7, pp. 22–49.
Noble, D. (1979), *America by Design* (Oxford: Oxford University Press).
Nugent, N., and King, R. (1977), *The British Right* (Farnborough: Saxon House).
Nun, J. (1967), 'The middle-class military coup', in *Politics of Conformity in Latin America*, ed. C. Veliz (London: Oxford University Press), pp. 66–118.
Offe, C., and Wiesenthal, H. (1980), 'Two logics of collective action: theoretical

notes on social class and organisational form', in *Political Power and Social Theory*, Vol. 1, ed. M. Zeitlin (Greenwich, Connecticut: Jai), pp. 67–115.

Oppenheimer, M. (1973), *The Proletarianisation of the Professional*, Sociological Review Monograph No. 20 (Keele: University of Keele), pp. 213–28.

Orwell, G. (1939), *Coming Up for Air* (London: Gollancz).

Pahl, J. M., and Pahl, R. E. (1971), *Managers and their Wives* (London: Allen Lane).

Parkin, F. (1968), *Middle Class Radicalism* (Manchester: Manchester University Press).

Parkin, F. (1972), *Class Inequality and Political Order* (London: Paladin).

Parkin, F. (1979), *Marxism and Class Theory: A Bourgeois Critique* (London: Tavistock).

Parry, N., and Parry, J. (1976), *The Rise of the Medical Profession* (London: Croom Helm).

PCF Traité (1971), *Traité marxiste de l'économie politique: le capitalisme monopoliste d'état* (Paris: Partie Communiste Française).

Penn, R. (1982), '"The contested terrain": a critique of R. C. Edwards' theory of working class fractions and politics', in *Organisational Studies Year Book*, Vol. 2, ed. D. Dunkerley and G. Salaman (London: Routledge & Kegan Paul).

Perkin, H. (1969), *The Origins of Modern English Society* (London: Routledge & Kegan Paul).

Perucci, R. (1973), 'In the service of man: radical movements in the professions', in *Professionalisation and Social Change*, ed. P. Halmos, Sociological Review Monograph No. 20 (Keele: University of Keele), pp. 179–94.

Poulantzas, N. (1973), *Political Power and Social Classes* (London: New Left Books).

Poulantzas, N. (1975), *Classes in Contemporary Capitalism* (London: New Left Books).

Poulantzas, N. (1977), 'The new petty bourgeoisie', in *Class and Class Structure*, ed. A. Hunt (London: Lawrence & Wishart), pp. 113–24.

Price, R., and Bain, G. S. (1976), 'Union growth revisited', *British Journal of Industrial Relations*, vol. 14, pp. 339–55.

Przeworski, A. (1977), 'Proletariat into a class: the process of class formation from Karl Kautsky's *The Class Struggle* to recent controversies', *Politics and Society*, vol. 7, pp. 343–401.

Przeworski, A. (1980), 'Social democracy as a historical phenomenon', *New Left Review*, vol. 122, pp. 27–58.

Radice, H. (ed.) (1975), *International Firms and Modern Imperialism* (Harmondsworth: Penguin).

Reader, W. J. (1966), *Professional Men* (London: Weidenfeld & Nicolson).

Reissman, L. (1970), 'The subject is class', *Sociology and Social Research*, vol. 54, pp. 293–305.

Renner, K. (1953), 'The service class', repr. in Bottomore and Goode (eds), op. cit., pp. 249–52.

Rhee, H. E. (1968), *Office Automation in Social Perspective* (Oxford: Blackwell).

Roberts, K., Cook, F. G., Clark, S. C., and Semeonoff, E. (1977), *The Fragmentary Class Structure* (London: Heinemann).

Roderick, G., and Stephens, M. (1981), 'The universities', in *Where Did We Go Wrong? Industry, Education and Economy of Victorian Britain*, ed. G. Roderick and M. Stephens (Falmer: University of Sussex), pp. 185–202.

Rosenberg, N. (1981), 'Marx as a student of technology', in *Science, Technology and the Labour Process*, ed. L. Levidow and B. Young (London: CSE Books), pp. 8–31.

Ross, G. (1978), 'Marxism and the new middle classes', *Theory and Society*, vol. 5, pp. 163–90.

Rosser, C., and Harris, C. (1966), *The Family and Social Change* (London: Routledge & Kegan Paul).

Rothblatt, S. (1968), *The Revolution of the Dons* (Cambridge: Cambridge University Press).

Routh, G. (1980), *Occupation and Pay in Great Britain* (London: Macmillan).

Rowbotham, S., Segal, L., and Wainwright, H. (1980), *Beyond the Fragments* (London: Merlin Press).

Rowse, A. L. (1931), *Politics and the Younger Generation* (London: Faber).

Runciman, W. G. (ed.) (1978), *Max Weber* (Cambridge: Cambridge University Press).

Sanderson, M. (1972), *The Universities and British Industry, 1850–1970* (London: Routledge & Kegan Paul).

Sassoon, A. S. (1980), *Gramsci's Politics* (London: Croom Helm).

Scott, J. (1979), *Corporation, Classes, and Capitalism* (London: Hutchinson).

Sengenberger, W. (1978), *Die gegenwartige Arbeitslosigkeit – auch ein Strukturproblem der Arbeitsmarkts* (Frankfurt and New York: Campus).

Shils, E. (1972), *The Intellectual and the Powers and other Essays* (Chicago: Chicago University Press).

Sofer, C. (1970), *Men in Mid-Career: A Study of British Managers and Technical Specialists* (Cambridge: Cambridge University Press).

Sohn-Rethel, A. (1978), *Intellectual and Manual Labour* (London: Macmillan).

Speier, H. (1952), *Social Order and the Risks of War* (New York: Stewart).

Stark, D. (1980), 'Class struggle and the transformation of the labour process', *Theory and Society*, vol. 9, pp. 89–130.

Stewart, A., Prandy, K., and Blackburn, R. M. (1980), *Occupations and Social Stratification* (London: Macmillan).

Syzmanski, A. (1979), 'A critique and extension of the PMC', in Walker (ed.), op. cit., pp. 49–65.

Taylor, F. W., (1947), *The Principles of Scientific Management* (New York: Harper).

Thompson, E. P. (1967), 'Time, work-discipline, and industrial capitalism', *Past and Present*, vol. 38, pp. 56–97.

Thompson, E. P. (1968), *The Making of the English Working Class* (Harmondsworth: Penguin).

Turner, B. S. (1977), 'The structuralist critique of Weber's sociology', *British Journal of Sociology*, vol. 28, pp. 1–16.

Turner, B. S. (1981), *For Weber* (London: Routledge & Kegan Paul).

Urry, J. (1973a), *Reference Groups and the Theory of Revolution* (London: Routledge & Kegan Paul).

Urry, J. (1973b), 'Towards a structural theory of the middle class', *Acta Sociologica*, vol. 16, pp. 175–87.

Urry, J. (1976), 'Nieuwe theorieen over die nieuwe middenklasse', *Amsterdams Sociologisch Tijdschrift*, vol. 4, pp. 68–85.

Urry, J. (1980), 'Paternalism, management and localities', Lancaster Regionalism Group Working Paper No. 2.

Urry, J. (1981a), 'Localities, regions and social class', *International Journal of Urban and Regional Research*, vol. 5, pp. 455–74.

Urry, J. (1981b), *The Anatomy of Capitalist Societies* (London: Macmillan).

Walker, P. (ed.) (1979), *Between Labour and Capital* (New York: Monthly Review).

Warner, L. W. (1960), *Social Class in America* (New York: Harper & Row).

Weber, M. (1964), *The Theory of Social and Economic Organisation* (New York: The Free Press).

Weber, W. (1975), *Music and the Middle Class* (London: Croom Helm).

Wells, H. G. (1905), *Kipps* (London: Odhams).

Wertheim, W. F. (1959), *Indonesian Society in Transition* (The Hague: Van Hoeve).

West, J. (1978), 'Women, sex, and class', in *Feminism and Marxism*, ed. A. Kuhn and A. M. Wolpe (London: Routledge & Kegan Paul), pp. 220–53.

Westergaard, J., and Resler, H. (1975), *Class in a Capitalist Society* (Harmondsworth: Penguin).

Wiener, M. J. (1981), *English Culture and the Decline of the Industrial Spirit, 1850–1980* (Cambridge: Cambridge University Press).

Williams, R. (1961), *Culture and Society, 1780–1950* (Harmondsworth: Penguin).

Williamson, J. (1974), *Late Nineteenth Century American Development* (Cambridge: Cambridge University Press).

Willis, P. (1977), *Learning to Labour* (Farnborough: Saxon House).

Woodward, J. (1960), *The Saleswomen* (London: Pitman).

Worsley, P. (1973), 'The distribution of power in industrial society', in *Power in Britain*, ed. J. Urry and J. Wakeford (London: Heinemann), pp. 247–65.

Wright, E. O. (1977), 'Class boundaries in advanced capitalist societies', *New Left Review*, vol. 98, pp. 3–41.

Wright, E. O. (1978), *Class, Crisis and the State* (London: New Left Books).

Wright, E. O., and Perrone, L. (1977), 'Marxist class categories and income inequality', *American Sociological Review*, vol. 42, pp. 32–55.

Yaffe, D., and Bullock, P. (1975), 'Inflation, the crisis and the post-war boom', *Revolutionary Communist*, vols 3–4, pp. 5–45.

Index

References in italics are to tables